THE BATTERED WOMAN'S SURVIVAL GUIDE

THE BATTERED WOMAN'S SURVIVAL GUIDE

BREAKING THE CYCLE

Jan Berliner Statman

Foreword by Sharon Obregon, MSSW
Executive Program Director, The Family Place

TAYLOR PUBLISHING COMPANY
DALLAS, TEXAS

Published by Taylor Publishing Company
1550 West Mockingbird Lane
Dallas, Texas 75235

Library of Congress Cataloging-in-Publication Data

Statman, Jan Berliner.
    The battered woman's survival guide: breaking the cycle/Jan
Berliner Statman.
        p.   cm.
    ISBN 0-87833-890-X: $18.95 — ISBN 0-87833-889-6 (pbk.): $9.95
    1. Abused women — United States. 2. Abused women — services for —
United States. I. Title.
HV6626.S72   1995
362.82'92 — dc20

                                                                89-20606
                                                                    CIP

Printed in the United States of America

10 9 8 7 6 5 4 3 2

This book is dedicated to all the wonderful men in my life: to the memory of my beloved father, Saul Berliner, whose loving heart and sweet nature knew no boundaries; to my dear husband, Max, whose world could never imagine such evil; and to our sons, Charles Barry and Louis Craig, who are the hope of the future.

And to the special women in my life: to my mother, Sylvia Berliner, who is the most remarkable woman I have ever known; to my brilliant sister, Donna; and to my daughter Sherry Michelle, who is so often perceptive beyond her years.

Contents

Foreword

In the early 1970s it would have taken courage for Jan Berliner Statman to publish *The Battered Woman's Survival Guide*. In all probability she would not have been aware that violence against women was the pervasive social problem that we now know it to be. It would have been so much more practical for her to have written a romantic novel about a hero and heroine—the latter who would have endured captivity, degradation, rejection, and torture because she believed that she was destined for true love.

For more than ten years I have had the opportunity to work with hundreds of battered women who sought refuge and help out of fear for their lives and the lives of their children. Even today, many of those women do not realize that they *are* battered, even though they have survived years of pain and abuse. Many of them do not realize that violence is not acceptable, that people aren't for hurting, and that they are not the cause of the violence.

One out of every four women in this country will experience ongoing, systematic episodes of violence within the context of loving relationships. Those relationships will not be romantic, and many will end in death or mutilation of body or spirit, or both. Society is beginning to realize that relationships are not fairy tales and that a good relationship requires skill, good mental health, and two people who are autonomous and who will continue growing throughout their lifetimes. The longer a woman remains in a relationship in which she is a victim, the harder it will be for her to recover that part of herself which she loses piece by piece. Education, reality, and a commitment to a non-violent society will ensure a better existence for today...but more importantly for the generations of tomorrow.

Sharon Obregon, MSSW
Executive Program Director
The Family Place

Part One

THE BATTERING RELATIONSHIP

1

The Unreported Epidemic

She Could Be Someone You Know

She could be your daughter, your sister, your neighbor, your friend. She could be a corporate executive, the saleswoman who sold you your new winter coat, a college professor, or a well-respected surgeon. She could be anyone. She could even be someone you love.

If it's hard to believe these women could be battered, keep reading. If someone you know is currently being battered, keep reading. In fact, if you are female or care about someone who is, keep reading.

Despite the popular misconceptions, battering does not happen exclusively to women who live "on the other side of the tracks." It does not happen exclusively to poor women or uneducated women. It is not exclusive to urban or rural women, to young or old women, to women of a particular color, race, or ethnicity. Battering happens to women who are single, married, divorced, child-blessed, and childless. Battering occurs everywhere, among every group.

The Extent of the Problem

Statistics indicate that one American woman out of every two will be physically abused at some time in her life by the man she loves and lives with. This means that if you are a woman, you have a 50-50 chance of being abused by your husband, your boyfriend, or your lover. *The Bureau of Justice National Crime Survey states that a woman is beaten in her home every 15 seconds.*

A study conducted by the March of Dimes indicates that one of every twelve women is battered while she is pregnant. Battered women are four times more likely to have low birthweight babies and are twice as likely to miscarry when compared with normal mothers. In fact, battering becomes increasingly frequent during pregnancy, when there are small children in the home, and when the children of the family become teenagers. It is a learned behavior; sons often follow their fathers' examples and beat their mothers and ultimately their wives.

Councils on Family Violence provide alarming statistics. Seventy percent of all emergency room assault cases are women. Twenty percent of all hospital emergency room visits by women are attributed to beatings. Battering is the single most significant cause of women's injuries, claiming more lives than muggings, rapes, or automobile accidents. Half of America's women are safer on the streets than they are in the "comfort" of their own homes. They are in greater danger of assault, violence, injury, and murder from members of their families than from strangers.

Twenty-five percent of all murders occur in the home and involve family members. Two thousand to four thousand battered women are beaten to death each year. A 1983 FBI Uniform Crime Report indicates that nearly one-third of female homicide victims are killed by their husbands or boyfriends. Ten percent of the men who are murdered in America each year are killed by their female partners acting in self-defense.

Councils on Family Violence are alarmed by how widespread the problem is. And although the statistics are shocking, they do not even begin to reveal the whole story. It is hard to know the exact figures since an estimated eighty percent of the cases of domestic violence go unreported because the battered women are ashamed, are mistakenly protecting their abusers, or are fearful of reprisals.

The Cycle of Violence

Such abuse has been called the most under-reported crime in America. Councils on Family Violence have labeled battering an "Unreported Epidemic." However, a battering relationship is not normal. Rather, violence is a learned behavior.

In studies of prison populations, The Texas League of Women Voters determined that ninety percent of all male inmates grew up in violent homes. Councils on Family Violence estimate that millions of American men are wife-batterers and that sixty percent of these men grew up in homes where they were the victims of family violence or watched as their mothers and sisters became the victims.

In addition, they estimate that approximately one-third to one-half of all batterers will abuse their children. Those who do not physically abuse their children are still guilty of a dangerous form of secondary child abuse. Consider the damage done to the minds and personalities of children forced to watch their fathers batter their mothers. Moreover, abusive men frequently beat, rape, or otherwise damage their young daughters, or daughters their wives bring into the home from former marriages. Homegrown violence is passed from generation to generation in an endless downward spiral.

The History of Domestic Violence

No one enters a romance intending to become a battered woman. When you look at the family albums of battered women, you usually find photographs that show happy, smiling, confident brides looking forward to lives of harmony and peace. You don't see pictures of black eyes, bruised limbs, and broken bones that may never be set.

What goes wrong?

We are just beginning to grapple with domestic violence in contemporary America. Wife beating was an accepted part of marriage in many countries until as late as the nineteenth century. From the early days of recorded history, some cultures had considered women to be their husbands' property. Roman men held the right of life and death over their wives. English common law allowed a husband to force his wife's obedience. The phrase "rule of thumb" derives from the "benevolent" English common law which restricted a man to beating his wife with "a whip or rattan no bigger than the width of his thumb."

Much of American law was based on English law. The so-called sanctity of the home excluded women from protection under the law until 1895 when the Married Women's Property Act made conviction for assault sufficient grounds for divorce. Although the burden of proof was so high that few women ever achieved such convictions, the act helped to change the concept of a wife as her husband's property. It laid the groundwork for twentieth-century legislation which grants married women the same protection under the law as other citizens.

One of the first women's shelters in America appeared in the small town of Belton, Texas, in 1866 when Martha White McWhirter founded the Sanctificationist religious group in the belief that no woman should live with an "unsanctified" or brutal husband. The women who followed her sought escape from their alcoholic and battering husbands. The "Belton Sanctificationists" worked together, pooling their resources and talents until, by the 1880s, the fifty women in the self-reliant group owned three farms, a steam laundry, a hotel, and several rooming houses. Irate husbands responded to the shelter with violence, even gunshots. Mrs. McWhirter's home still stands in Belton, Texas, with a bullet hole in its front door.

In spite of legislation enacted to protect women, the legal system still has a hard time dealing with domestic violence. The batterer can still hide behind closed doors and wrap himself in the cloak of respectability. Women are still silenced by shame while society sanctimoniously turns its back.

But the situation is changing. In 1970 there was no place for battered women to go. Today there are more than twelve hundred shelters and service programs across the country. Although this does not comprise a shelter in every city, county, and town or for every battered woman who needs one, it is a giant step forward.

Furthermore, most Americans are good and decent people. We are unwilling to stand idly by and watch as the women in our neighborhoods, our churches, and our lives are abused, brutally beaten, and even murdered. We simply need to know what signs to watch for. And we need to know what to do when we see them. By learning more about batterers and the battering relationship, we can find ways to help battered women.

Examining the myths which allow battering to flourish in our society is a good way to begin.

Myths of Romance

Most of us were brought up on a rich diet of myths and fairy tales. Cinderella, Sleeping Beauty, Rapunzel, and Snow White were beautiful, passive women who waited in a castle, forest, or ivory tower for Prince Charming to show up and bring them true love or otherwise make their unhappy lives work. Unfortunately, certain warning signs of potentially battering relationships may be mis-interpreted because of such storybook ideas about "true love" and idyllic romance.

For example, there is the idea that the only way a woman can survive is by pleasing a man. Some women do survive this way, but only because the man they love is capable of being pleased. The batterer is not. There is the notion that "all's fair in love and war." This promotes the idea that marriage is such a private relationship that law enforcement agencies and legal systems should stay out of the picture—even if the picture includes assault and potential murder. There is the idea that "making up is the best part of a fight," a romantic notion which loses its validity when the woman must "make up" from a hospital bed. And then there is the idea that a woman should keep her family together for the children's sake. Yet children are better off with one sane parent than with two seriously damaged parents, or with a parent who completely controls, subordinates, dominates, abuses, and perhaps finally murders the other.

Modern romances only reinforce the fairy tales beloved by our culture. In movie romances, love is a song and dance. In pulp magazines, love ends all pain. In TV specials, the hero and the heroine live happily ever after. There is even a genre of romantic novels and historical romances known as "bodice rippers." These can be identified by covers which depict devastatingly handsome, bare-chested men, variously dressed as pirates, English gentlemen, or gallant gypsies, and nibbling the necks of scantily clad women.

These paperbacks, sold at grocery store checkout counters, almost always tell the story of a brave but domineering man. He loves a submissive woman, although his unfortunate background renders him incapable of telling her how much he cares. In fact, it causes him to treat her quite badly through most of the book. But, true love conquers all. They marry in the final chapter and presumably live happily ever after.

Real life doesn't work like that. If a man mistreats a woman at the beginning of their relationship, he will mistreat her after they are married. Marriage will only make it worse, usually *much* worse.

Finally, the romantic myth that true lovers are never apart renders one of the batterer's most common behaviors confusing to the woman involved. Our literature tells of true lovers who expire when they are not together. Romeo and Juliet, for example, could not face life without each other. But Romeo would never have demanded that Juliet agree to his total, unconditional, oppressive demands on every hour of her life.

There is nothing romantic about unreal demands or mental or physical abuse. Real life romance involves mutual trust, respect, and understanding. Nobody has to "take the bad with the good" when the bad includes battering.

Who Becomes a Battered Woman?

Who can become a battered woman? Any woman. Psychologists have never been able to isolate a common denominator among battered women. In fact, most sociologists agree that seeking a common denominator puts the blame for this epidemic on the victims.

Some battered women are beautiful, some are plain. Some are bright and some are not. Some are outgoing while others are retiring. They are rich, poor, and middle class. Some are sophisticated while others are innocent. Some come from broken homes while others grew up in warm, loving families.

If there *is* any common denominator among battered women, it may be their trusting natures. They are frequently nonaggressive and traditional. They may have been brought up to believe that a man should be the master of his household, or that a man is a king in his own home. Because of this, they may accept the guilt for what has happened to their lives. They may appear calm to others while denying the anger and terror they feel. They often have low self-esteem to begin with, or self-esteem that has been temporarily shattered by events, causing them to be vulnerable to the batterer at a particular time. This vulnerability may be evident in very young women, or it may be the result of the death of a parent or loved one, a divorce, the loss of a job, a significant career change, or even an emotional upheaval such as the clanging of the biological clock.

A batterer will unerringly "zero in" on the most vulnerable woman in any room.

What Kind of Man Beats a Woman?

Batterers also come from all racial, ethnic, social, and cultural levels. They too are as varied as the individual circumstances in which they live. Some men become short-term batterers as a way of acting out their rage toward adverse circumstances. Their lack of control over unemployment or business failures leads them to batter the weakest, most defenseless person in their lives. Others are long-term batterers who always beat their women and often have a long history of criminal activities.

Batterers are easy to spot when you know what characteristics to look for. These are covered in detail in the next chapter. All women and girls should be aware of these tell tale signs before becoming involved in a romantic relationship.

First, a man who is a batterer was probably physically or psychologically abused in his home as a child, or he grew up in a violent home in which his father beat or completely dominated his mother. Of course this was really unfortunate for him. But a woman who is attracted to him must keep in mind that his unfortunate childhood was and is his problem, not hers. If she tries to nurture, care for, and protect him, he will systematically erode her personality and use her for a punching bag.

Second, batterers are usually manipulative and often exhibit a "Dr. Jekyll and Mr. Hyde" personality. They can be pleasant and charming one minute, aggressive and violent the next. A woman who is involved with a batterer never knows which behavior he will exhibit and finds herself walking on eggs to keep him calm and to protect herself.

Even if nothing about his childhood is known, and his dual personality has not surfaced, a woman should suspect any man who abuses alcohol and/or drugs. He will always insist that he is merely a "social drinker" or a "social user," because that is what he chooses to believe. But if he ever becomes angry or abusive when he is using alcohol or drugs, she will be in real danger.

Research into the psychological causes of battering behavior is just beginning. Most battering men refuse to acknowledge that they have a problem. And in one sense, they *don't*. What they seek is control, and their control is complete. Since most men are larger and stronger than most women, the batterer is in little danger from physical retribution. In fact, a battered woman's attempts to protect herself by fighting off her partner's assault often enrage him and intensify the battering. Since he does not suffer physically or emotionally from the consequences of his violence, a batterer almost never voluntarily comes forward for help until after the woman has left or sought help. If she is unwilling or unable to leave or seek help, her partner has no incentive for changing his behavior.

The assumption that batterers want domestic harmony in their lives is not necessarily correct. Some of them may actually experience pain and grief or psychological discomfort when their women eventually leave them. However, since they are often manipulative, the emotions they display may not be real. A few actually go for counseling to help them overcome their violence. Some act loving and contrite, making effusive promises and begging the woman to return. Some become aggressive and violent, doing everything in their power to force her back. Others simply shrug off the loss and move on to batter another and still another woman.

Recognizing a Woman Who is Being Battered
If you are not a battered woman, but have a family member you suspect is, what can you do? How can you even recognize a battered woman?

If a woman is frequently absent from work or social activities and if she reappears wearing extremely heavy makeup, sunglasses indoors, long sleeves in warm weather, or scarves around her throat, suspect battering. If her face seems swollen, if her arms are bruised, if she has difficulty articulating or chewing solid food, and if her husband's presence seems intrusive or oppressive, suspect battering.

If a woman has a remarkable incidence of sickness, "psychosomatic" ailments, or surgeries, suspect battering. Curiously, some of the most vicious batterers become gentle, kind, and nurturing when their partners are ill. Since the batterer can completely control the woman's actions and decisions when she is sick and helpless, he feels free to comfort her. He spares her from battering, and from his perfectionistic demands, and may even shower her with attention and affection . . . until the moment she recovers.

If a woman's personality has changed, it is not unreasonable to suspect battering. A formerly vivacious or opinionated woman may suddenly become vacant or noncommittal. She may seem afraid to contact old friends. She may seem excessively private. She may hide things or ask others to perform common tasks like calling a creditor or a physician for her. If she cannot hide black eyes, broken limbs, or obvious bruises and if she is confronted directly about her bruises, she will probably say she was in an auto accident, or fell off a chair, or tripped, or walked into a door.

Remember, the woman is terrified, she has been brainwashed, and she may even continue to love the charming Dr. Jekyll side of the batterer's personality.

Helping Her to Protect Herself

If she became a battered woman, remember that although she has become a victim, she has not done anything to "deserve" this mistreatment.

She has not brought this on herself. He has.

She has not displayed a flawed personality. He has.

She has not brought out the worst in him. He has.

If you suspect battering and the woman does not or cannot admit she is in danger, bear in mind that she is suffering from learned helplessness. She may be convinced that she must rely on the batterer to survive. Also, she knows that he may choose to kill her rather than permit her to leave. Share your kindness, your thoughts, and your information with her, but respect her decisions and her timing. If she will take it, give her the address and telephone number of the nearest family crisis center.

And never forget: *She really is in life-threatening danger.*

Professionals will frequently tell concerned friends, family, and associates that there is nothing anyone can do to help a battered woman until she asks for help. But can you really afford to turn away from her suffering? When Rabbi Dennis Math of the Village Temple in New York gave the eulogy at the funeral of little Lisa Steinberg, he addressed the problem of battering and suggested an answer.

He said, "We permit people to pursue their freedom as long as their freedom does not infringe on ours. But maybe we should question this tolerant attitude.

"In the Torah. . .we are told to rebuke our neighbor. It is implied that what our neighbor is doing is our concern. Perhaps we have learned in a tragic way that our respect for our neighbor's privacy must not be as important as other considerations. When we hear that a person is being harmed, we cannot be respectful of our neighbor's . . . privacy. We must risk even being wrong, being embarrassed, and even evoking a neighbor's anger . . ."

Even though caring friends and relatives may not be allowed to do anything concrete to help a battered woman until she asks for help (they may not even be allowed to force her to go to the hospital to get treatment for her injuries if she doesn't want to go), it is possible—it is essential—to find a way to encourage her to ask for help. Every situation is different; therefore finding exactly the correct way to help each battered woman will be different. But friends, relatives, and counselors must be ready and available to do what needs to be done. Here are some things that can be done to help a battered woman who has not yet asked for help:

1. Find a safe way for her to read this book. It has the information she needs to save herself. But don't let her take it home where the batterer can find it and punish her for reading it. You may have to invent a way to let her read it in a safe place: at your house, at a friend or relative's house, or at the library. If she is a student, give her time to read this book at school. If she is an employee, give her time to read this book at work. If she is a patient, ask her to read it in your office. If she is a congregant, find a way for her to read it in the privacy of a religious environment.

2. Give her the telephone number of the local battered women's shelter. Or give her the telephone number of the National Domestic Violence Hotline (1-800-333-SAFE). Tell her to call when she is ready to be helped.

3. Don't forget her. Don't give up on her. Don't abandon her. Let her know that you care about her even if she says she doesn't care about you.

4. Keep in touch with her even if talking to her is painful to you. Call her and keep calling her. Call her even if you have to talk to the batterer. Call her even if she hangs up on you. Find a way to see her even if she doesn't let you come into her house. The

batterer is trying to isolate her from familiar people and surroundings. Don't let it happen to her. She is drowning in a world she cannot control. Hang on to her for dear life! You may be her only lifeline back to the sane and normal world.

5. If she is enduring total surveillance by her batterer, keep trying until you find a way to speak to her alone. You may have to enlist the help of the men in your family or social group to "entertain" the batterer, whether this means whisking him away for a trip to the local bar after Thanksgiving dinner or dragging him off to the back porch for "men's talk." Do anything that will give you the opportunity to speak with her alone, even briefly. She may not appear to respond to you, but somewhere in the back of her mind, she will remember. The opportunity to breathe clearly for even a few minutes may make the difference between denial and admittance.

6. Make her aware of her options. Remind her of her skills, her talents, and her abilities. Remind her of jobs she may have held and successes she may have achieved. Keep reminding her that there is a sane and normal world waiting for her return.

7. Let her know you are willing to help her in a concrete way, and tell her what you are willing to do, whether it is offering financial help, a place for her to stay, or a ride to the women's shelter.

8. Remember, she has been carefully and systematically brainwashed by the batterer. Don't expect her to change overnight. Don't expect her to ask for help today or even tomorrow. Miracles seldom happen overnight. You must be patient, kind, caring, and, most of all, you must be as tenacious as a dog with a bone. Don't let up and don't let go. And you must be willing and ready to help her the very first time she asks for help.

Domestic Violence Can Be Stopped

Battered women and battered families are indeed an unreported epidemic. But our society's violence against women can be stopped. It is a crime and it should be treated as such. It is essential to educate the entire nation about how widespread family violence is. It is essential to help battered women who are in danger. It is essential to provide community services such as counseling, support groups, crisis intervention services, and shelters for battered women and their children. It is essential to provide legal advocacy and legal defenses for the defenseless. It will take a lot of courage from the battered women and from society as well. But millions of American men and women are living in a war zone.

All of us can do better.

2

How Did This Happen?

THE ANATOMY AND PROGRESS OF
AN ABUSIVE RELATIONSHIP

How Did She Get Into This?

A battering relationship begins the moment a batterer's internal "radar" somehow seeks out a woman who is vulnerable at that particular moment in her life. He may charm her or "sweep her off her feet" in the storybook sense. He may send bouquets of flowers to her home and to her place of business. He may call her at any hour, even every hour on the hour, "just to hear her voice." He may appear thoroughly devoted to her. He may even present himself as the Prince Charming who can carry her off to live happily ever after in his castle in the clouds.

He will probably convince her that he is the most capable, dynamic, and competent man she has ever known, that he is exactly the man who can take charge of her life, the man she can believe in, the man of her dreams. His manipulative personality will enable him to discover her fondest desires and echo her conversations, making her think he totally shares her interests. He may overwhelm her with largely unsubstantiated stories about his wealth, power, success, or fame. It would be wise for her to remember that if a man seems too good to be true, he probably is.

Is This Prince Charming or a Potential Batterer?

A batterer can be hard to detect at the onset of a relationship, but the true stories in Part II demonstrate that domestic violence builds in a clear, characteristic pattern. It is as if all batterers read the same imaginary handbook of techniques to help them promote their violence. The woman is effectively brainwashed through a series of steps described in detail in this chapter.

The batterer degrades her into believing that she is incompetent and incapable of managing the simplest tasks of daily life or personal interaction. When she expresses dissatisfaction or unhappiness, he convinces her she is to blame. He makes her believe that if she would only change, if she would only do as he says, their life together would be as perfect and as happy as they know it can be. He will create most, if not all, of the following circumstances:

Separation
Surveillance
Exhaustion and Hunger
Hostility and Paranoia
Chemical Dependence
Financial Dependence
Financial Deprivation
Discredit
Insecurity
Battering
A Cycle of Violence
Sexual Abuse
Guilt and Denial

Separation

Once the relationship is established, the batterer will do everything possible to separate his victim from her support system of friends and family. He may isolate her by repeatedly making appointments with the people she loves and respects, only to cancel them at the last moment. He may do this through broken promises, or by becoming involved in bitter disagreements with her nearest and dearest so he can demand that she choose between him and them. He will distort her understanding of reality by constantly insisting that her friends and family are enemies of their relationship and blaming them for the couple's unhappiness.

How Did This Happen?

He will tell her that her friends and family have used her for their own selfish ends in the past, and that they will continue to do so unless he protects her. He will say he is the only one in the world who cares for her as she should be cared for. He will tell her, and perhaps her astonished family, that he will not allow them to continue mistreating her or making her unhappy.

He will attempt to destroy her confidence in those she loves by saying things like, "They are your enemies, I am your only friend. They are jealous of us, of our love, of our relationship, of what we have together. They want to use you for their own purposes. I am the only one in the world who loves you un-selfishly," or "I am the only one who cares about you and truly wishes to see you happy."

When family or friends persist in including her in celebrations, gatherings, and holidays, or in sharing her company, when they refuse to engage in his arguments, or try to disclose his fantasies for what they are, or when they protest against his unfounded allegations, he may tell them, "I will not allow you to continue to ruin her life!" or "I will not allow you to make her unhappy," or "I will not allow you to do this to her any longer."

She is a grown-up. She should know who her real friends are, but he will insist that it is necessary for him to separate her from these people "for her own good" or for reasons of her health or safety. He may tell her it is necessary to separate her from them to protect their relationship from the threats posed by outsiders. He will convince her that even though it troubles him, he is doing what is best for her happiness.

None of this is true. He is a terrorist and he is setting up the first step on her journey into chaos.

Sometimes he is suspicious of any conversation she has with anyone under any circumstances and demands to know every word that is said. He may even insist upon listening in or recording all her telephone conversations. This makes communication difficult at best, and actually dangerous for her. The battered woman, her friends or family, or possibly all concerned, may find that keeping in contact becomes so difficult and has such dangerous consequences that it is easier to simply give up. If long-time friends and family members are not permitted to talk with a woman alone, chances are she is being battered.

He will find a reason to move to another city, state, or

community, or to an isolated area where she will not only be separated from her personal support group and business contacts, but from her normal and familiar surroundings as well. He will do this under some pretext that seems convincing at the time, and which may be acceptable or even admirable to her friends and family. He may say the move offers a better job, a larger house, or better social standing. But afterward she is isolated and becomes increasingly dependent on him for human contact. This is particularly insidious because her unhealthy interaction with him replaces truly normal ways of relating to other people. She probably has to account for every penny she spends so that making long-distance calls to those she left behind is difficult or impossible.

By the time her family and friends realize something is very wrong, it may be too late. Her partner may have begun to bluster and brag constantly or he may have become argumentative, even quarrelsome. He will have begun to dominate her and will attempt to dominate conversations and situations. He will have become sufficiently offensive that her family and friends would prefer to avoid his company. They may even feel that they should protect her from him, but if they don't understand what is really going on, they won't know exactly how to help her.

They must find a way. She is in danger, and she cannot help herself.

Surveillance

The batterer is manipulative, domineering, and demanding. He expects his woman to keep him informed of her whereabouts at all times. This can be accomplished in many ways, but what starts out as a seemingly gentle, romantic request soon escalates into an oppressive, tyrannical demand. The woman is persuaded to leave her job in order to spend all her time where he can watch her. The abusive man says he absolutely *needs* her constant presence. If he cannot force her to quit her job, he may appear at her place of work so often that he makes it impossible for her to do her job. He may insist on taking her to work, meeting her for lunch, seeing or telephoning her on her breaks, and picking her up after work, often arriving thirty minutes to an hour early and waiting in a prominent location that is irritating to her employer.

If she is not employed, he will ask her to appear at his

workplace with something he needs or forgets in the morning, with his lunch at noon, with something else in the afternoon, and then immediately after work. He may even convince her that he needs her help with his business and manipulate her into being at his beck and call twenty-four hours a day.

He will tell her that he "loves her so much" that he cannot bear for them to be apart. Perhaps this is true love and abiding romance. Or perhaps it is calculated to separate the woman from everyone and everything she knows and oblige her to tolerate his excessive demands and eventually his brutality.

Inordinate and often delusional jealousy also characterize the batterer. While the fact is that most battered women are simply so physically and emotionally exhausted that the last thing in the world they are interested in is an affair or even a casual flirtation, the batterer will accuse her of every form of seductive behavior. He may criticize her walk, mannerisms, conversation, or clothing. The batterer's accusations seem to come out of nowhere.

Suspicion about her relationships with other men is not the only form his jealousy takes. He may be jealous of family, friends, the family pet, small children, the employer, colleagues, or strangers. He can be set off by anything at all . . . or by nothing. Perhaps she prepares a meal he particularly enjoys, or dislikes. Perhaps she questions the taste of a cup of restaurant coffee. Or perhaps a friend or relative calls on the phone. In some cases he can exhibit paranoid symptoms, insisting that they are being watched or followed, or that mysterious others are attempting to break up their relationship. He may try to convince her that he is being followed or that some evil force is "against" him and he must forever be alert, protecting himself with guns, knives, or other weapons.

One particularly eerie aspect of many a batterer's behavior is the verbal abuse during which the woman becomes a mirror of his own failures and inadequacies. A batterer may accuse his partner of pathological lying, incompetence, stupidity, or socially unacceptable behavior. He may accuse her of infidelity with others when that is what he is involved in. He probably tells her she is sexually incompetent in one way or another, that she cannot retain interpersonal relationships, that her parents do not and have never loved her properly, that she has no empathy for others, and that she publicly embarrasses him.

Exhaustion and Hunger

Once she has been separated from her lifelong support system of family and friends, the batterer will find a way to keep the woman exhausted and/or hungry. He may deprive her of sleep or food. He may insist on keeping very late hours and awaken her in the middle of the night or early in the morning. He may involve her in a project such as building a new home or starting a new business, or keep her overwhelmed with social or business activity which requires long hours or intensive physical labor. All of this activity has come about totally by his choice—not hers. She is so exhausted and/or so hungry, she can't think clearly. Her thinking becomes chaotic.

His Hostility and Paranoia

It is possible that he will become violent, verbally abusive, or extremely defensive with others. He may throw food, break furniture, burn or tear up her clothing, and threaten not only her life but the lives of her children and extended family as well. He may become enraged when his plans are changed in any way. He may have a distorted view of reality. He may even be charming in public yet brutal in private. Through a combination of tactics, the batterer confuses the woman so thoroughly that she begins to depend on him to define reality. If she somehow manages to maintain her own reality, she will realize that she is living in a world of nightmarish distortions.

Chemical Dependence

The batterer will often encourage a woman to become drug or alcohol dependent as a way to control her and to keep her dependent upon him as the source for providing drugs and/or alcohol. This is particularly prevalent when the batterer himself abuses drugs or alcohol. He may insist that she accompany him on his binges. If she refuses, he may resort to adding drugs or alcohol to her food and drink without her knowledge.

Financial Dependence

Since his goal is to achieve total control of his victim, the batterer will seek to make her financially as well as emotionally dependent upon him. If she is a corporate executive, she will turn her paycheck over to him. If she is a surgeon or a part-time clerical, she will do the same thing.

He may convince her to quit her job and stop seeing her former associates, colleagues, or co-workers. He may not permit her to work in a situation where she can control her own money by telling her that he is the provider for the family and he would be devastated if she had a "menial" job. He may convince her that he is so wealthy she no longer needs to work outside the home. Or he may insist that her working outside the home hurts his pride or his community standing.

Once she stops working and no longer has an income, he will convince her to spend any money she saved before their relationship for such apparently acceptable purposes as an elaborate wedding, a dream vacation trip, a house, a car, a boat, or some other luxury. If the purchase is real property, it will always be purchased with her money but he will insist that it be in his name as "head of the household." Or he will convince her to make a down payment on a large purchase such as a car or house-full of furniture. He will then default on the payments, so that the ensuing repossession will destroy her hard-earned credit record. She probably won't know about the default until a repossession company comes to take the car or furniture away, since by now he is hiding most of her mail.

Financial Deprivation

When she becomes financially dependent upon him, money will become a real and overwhelming issue in her life because no matter what he earns, he will see to it that she never has enough to make ends meet. Even the rich are battered, and even very wealthy women are kept penniless.

The batterer will take out as much money as he wants, then make a great issue of turning the remainder of his paycheck over to his victim. This will often not be sufficient to cover everyday household expenses, to pay regular bills, or to provide her with pocket money. He will demand to know exactly where every penny was spent and why. And he will become furious when she can't manage to provide for the normal household expenses or pay the regular bills with what money he has given her.

He will somehow prevent her from having transportation. He may sabotage her car or convince her that as a couple or family they only need one vehicle. He may remove her distributor cap or spark plugs when she needs to drive. Or he may simply have her car towed away.

At this stage, the woman will find that she is spending little, if anything, on herself. She never buys new clothes, she has begun looking bedraggled, and her clothes appear shabby or even dirty because she cannot afford dry cleaning. A previously fastidious woman will begin to wear torn pantyhose and rundown shoes. She may cut her own hair rather than go to the beauty shop. Possibly she no longer wears expensive makeup.

Whatever the particulars, she looks different, and worse.

Discredit

Once she leaves her job or profession, the batterer will make sure that she is unable to return. He will probably involve her in some form of social, professional, or business disgrace, perhaps by hinting at misconduct or unethical behavior, scandal, or even illegal activity.

It is not uncommon for batterers to manipulate their partners into real legal difficulties. She may be forced, at knife or gun-point if necessary, to sign hot checks. Or he may contrive to involve her in illicit drug-related activity, in illegal gambling, or in minor or major theft for which a warrant may be issued for her arrest.

He will steal her credit cards, confiscate her mail, and hide the bills for purchases he has made in her name and on her credit cards. He will sabotage her tax returns. When this happens, she is in trouble with creditors and with the law. She is completely at his mercy. He is her "protector" and her "guardian." She is obliged to go where he tells her and to do what he tells her. Not only must she find a way to survive, but she must do so in a legal pressure-cooker.

The sooner she calls a stop to this terror and retakes control, the less complicated her life will be.

Insecurity

Even the strongest person becomes vulnerable when she is alone in unfamiliar surroundings. Her vulnerability will be enforced as he begins to convince her that she is the cause of everything wrong in their relationship, including his abusive behavior. As she begins to doubt that she ever had a mind, he will keep undermining her flagging self-confidence. He will convince her that she is stupid and ugly, incompetent to deal with even the most elementary situations without his help and guidance.

As she becomes more and more insecure, she becomes more and more dependent upon him.

Battering

Once she is separated from her friends and family, located in unfamiliar surroundings, convinced she is incompetent to function fully as an adult, and dependent on him for all her needs, she is truly his hostage. Now the physical violence begins.

Battering typically starts with irrational arguments followed by mild threats. It escalates to shoving, then pushing, hitting, and slapping. It grows progressively more severe until it includes hitting with heavy objects, using or threatening to use guns, knives, or other weapons, and choking, stabbing, and other life-threatening acts. Somehow, she still thinks she can use reason or logic to make him stop.

This is unreasonable and illogical. She never made him start. She cannot make him stop.

A Cycle of Violence

Characteristically, councils on family violence recognize a three-phase cycle in abusive relationships. Although the cycle affords the woman brief periods of relief from the tortuous conditions under which she lives, it also makes it harder for her to break up the relationship.

The core of the relationship is denial. The batterer denies to himself and to his partner that he is abusive, unkind, irrational, unfair, or anything less than the perfect partner. The abused woman protects herself and the relationship by denying that she is abused or that anything is amiss in their "perfect" life together.

The first phase of the battering cycle takes up most of their mutual time together. During it, tension mounts and brief battering incidents may take place. Both the batterer and the victim know that a violent incident will take place. He grows more angry and irrational. She becomes more acquiescent and submissive. She does everything possible to try to avoid the battering, to calm his growing rage. Many battered women describe their behavior during this phase, as "walking on eggs." No matter what she does or does not do, a battering incident will happen.

In the second phase, there is an acute battering incident which begins and progresses with increased violence. It can last an hour, two hours, several days, or as long as it takes for the man's uncontrollable rage to subside. It may be interrupted as he leaves the house for several hours and then returns to batter her repeatedly.

Finally, the third or "honeymoon" phase of the battering cycle occurs. During this phase, the batterer reverts to his charming self, showing remorse and repentance. He promises to change, swears he will never batter her again, and showers her with affection, love, and gifts. He swears that he loves her and seems genuinely remorseful and apologetic.

Even though she knows this is not true, she desperately wants to believe his empty promises because she loves the Jekyll aspect of her partner's Jekyll and Hyde personality. Having been emotionally drained and physically tortured, she has few inner resources left and is in terrible pain. She falls into his arms with relief and comfort to be praised and assured of his love and protectiveness.

In her depleted state, this binds her more closely to him and firmly establishes her need to deny his abusive behavior. Where else would she get support? During this stage, she will usually deny the battering . . . even to herself.

She will find herself minimizing her injuries. She may not seek medical attention because she is in a state of shock and disbelief about what has happened to her. She begins to block out of consciousness the fact that she has been criminally assaulted by the same man who is now "loving" her. And once it starts, the cycle repeats itself with alarming regularity. It becomes the habit of life, and instinct replaces rationality. She does not leave because her thinking processes are geared only to moment-to-moment survival.

The best way to understand the battering cycle is to imagine that the battered woman is riding a carousel located inside a round building. The walls of the building are divided wedge-shaped thirds. One third of the wall is painted grey, representing the first stage of the battering cycle, when the woman knows that a serious battering incident is going to take place and finds herself walking on eggs to prevent it. The second third is painted blood red to represent the battering incident. The third part is painted heavenly blue to represent the honeymoon phase during which she denies how severe the battering is and his charm binds her more closely to him.

But remember: the building is round and the carousel moves on. As soon as she passes the blue wall, she heads directly for the grey wall. That takes her right back into the blood-red battering zone. It happens over and over and over.

The batterer is in control of the carousel—and of her life.

Sexual Demands, Sexual Violence, and Sexual Peculiarities

The batterer's sexual preferences usually have little to do with love and affection and a lot to do with dominance and subjugation. Sex on demand, rape, and brutal, violent, or degrading sexual acts may be a part of the batterer's repertoire as he psychologically and physically destroys his victim. He may be a gentle, exciting, and outstanding lover one time and a vicious, raging brute the next. He may insist on dressing up in her clothes. He may mutilate her. He may force her to have sex with other men. He may make extra money by selling her to other men. He may take compromising photographs of her, then blackmail her by threatening to show them to her employer or family if she leaves him. He may even make up lies about her, calling her bisexual, a lesbian, or a nymphomaniac, or saying she has worked as a prostitute, and threaten to make these stories public if she leaves him. Some batterers actually do make these stories and photographs public after the woman has escaped.

Guilt and Denial

The battered woman is ashamed of what has become of her relationship and her life. Traditionally, women are trained to be the homemakers and the mediators of domestic peace. Unable to fulfill this role satisfactorily, the battered woman feels that her life role as wife and mother is threatened. Because she feels ashamed and guilty, she may attempt to keep her batterer's violence secret.

Many a battered woman wants to leave her abusive relationship but has learned how to be a victim. She has learned helplessness, and in doing so has developed a paralysis of will.

Ashamed of what has happened to her, overwhelmed by fear and guilt, and made to feel that she is responsible for her own abuse, the battered woman begins to accept responsibility for causing his anger. Typically, she denies to outsiders that anything is wrong in her life. She protects the batterer by lying about her bruises or injuries. If her injuries are life-threatening or severe enough to require medical attention (and if the batterer allows her to receive medical attention), he expects her to make excuses to medical personnel and to attribute her injuries to accidental causes. She may explain a broken jaw by saying, "I fell off a ladder," or a broken arm by saying, "Clumsy me, the floor was wet and I slipped."

More dangerous than denying to other people what he has done, she begins to deny it to herself. She will not seek medical attention for days or even weeks. She endures the most unbearable physical pain, and then is astonished to discover that she has suffered broken bones or torn ligaments during his latest assault.

Even when she knows how bad the assault was, the battered woman tells herself that "it wasn't so bad," or that he "really did not intend to hurt me." She tells herself that her injuries did not happen because he hit her, but because she hurt herself when she fell. By doing this she assumes the blame for the injury. She denies that he has been cruel to her because she cannot stand to believe that the man she loves and lives with could hurt her so badly. And because of this denial, she does not realize that she has lost control of her own life.

Guilt is an element which cannot be ignored. The batterer says and does things which make the woman accept feelings of guilt for causing the abuse in their relationship. He tells her this is "all her fault" or that she is in some way to blame for his abusive behavior. In her dependent state, she is ashamed that she cannot be a better wife, a better housekeeper, a better mother, or better at any of the things that might somehow make him stop battering her.

Society reinforces the burden of guilt when it assumes that she has done something so bad that it *caused* her partner to abuse her. Society believes that it is a woman's inappropriate behavior which provokes the attacks on her, rather than condemning the batterer's bizarre behavior. Battered women will hear questions like, "What did you do to him to make him attack you?" Or, "You must have done something terrible to him to make him angry enough to hit you."

Still worse is the double-edged sword by which society blames the woman for not ending the battering relationship, while at the same time blaming her if she does end the relationship by saying that she has "destroyed her family."

This comes from normal people who are living normal lives in normal relationships where causes have effects. To a battered woman, it does not apply.

Learned Helplessness

In insidious ways, the woman is thus "brainwashed." Her independence is eroded. Her perception of reality is distorted. Her self-confidence is undermined. She learns how to be helpless. She learns to be a victim. Learned helplessness is part of the Battered Woman Syndrome and it is a behavior modification tactic. To explain it simply, remember that most of us expect certain responses when we do certain things. When the expected responses do not come, we consciously or unconsciously alter our behavior in order to elicit the desired response.

For example, we expect that if we go to the mailbox, it will contain mail addressed to us or to our family. We also know that the letter carrier will pick up and deliver our mail at a certain time of day.

Suppose you go to the mailbox to pick up your mail at the appropriate time and discover that your outgoing mail has not been picked up but your mailbox has been filled with mail addressed to other people. You call the post office to inquire about the problem and are told that the mail will only be picked up if a large red flag is attached to the mailbox. You go to the hardware store and buy a large red flag so that you may comply with the instructions, but your mail is still not picked up and other people's mail continues to appear in your mailbox.

You call the post office, and you are told that your envelopes must be of a certain size. You rush to the nearest stationery store to buy new envelopes. But your mail is still not picked up. Now you call the post office and are told that the problem has been solved. But you can look through your window to see a blizzard of papers, parcels, magazines, and postcards spreading across your lawn and into the street.

You complain that the problem has not been solved and you are told to use envelopes of a certain color as well as size. You rush to the stationery store to purchase the new envelopes, but the situation continues to become worse.

You don't receive any of the birthday cards or bills addressed to you, but more and more mail for more and more other people is stuffed into your box. You attempt to pick up all the mail and deliver it to the correct recipients, but the more you deliver the more mail arrives until the task becomes overwhelming. You have no control over the situation. You have no choices. You give up.

Now, imagine this problem applied to domestic life. No matter what the battered woman says or does, she cannot control her life. Her behavior does not bring a normal, predictable response. Second-guessing the response consumes every waking hour and every minute of her time until the woman finally gives up. Since she is helpless to cause her partner to respond in a normal way, she believes she is also helpless to conduct her life.

Why Doesn't She Just Leave?

The battered woman's friends and family usually cannot understand why she does not simply walk away and end the relationship, ask for help, or act to change her situation. Since she will not or cannot ask for help, they may feel overwhelmed. They may be confused and angry. They are convinced that they can't help her unless she asks.

Unless they have personally experienced an abusive relationship, those who care about her cannot understand what she is experiencing. She may hear them saying things like, "She must really love him to put up with that abuse," or "She must like being beaten or else she'd do something about it," or "She's a big girl. She can change her life if she wants to," or "If she's not happy about it, why doesn't she simply pack up and leave him?"

The answer is that, at this moment, she cannot. She has been brainwashed. Her image of herself has been virtually destroyed. She has been taught that she is ugly, incapable, and incompetent. Her personality has been carefully and conscientiously eroded. Her will has been paralyzed. Her perceptions of reality are seriously skewed.

Even if she can somehow work up the courage to escape, she may have no idea where to turn or where to find help. She cannot live in the street. She has no job. She has no money. Worse, her friends and family may be unwilling or unable to offer her shelter. They may fear reprisals from her violent partner, have strong religious convictions which exclude her, or simply be unwilling to get involved in her private affairs. They may even have sheltered her when she left the batterer before only to see her return to the batterer. Friends and family simply don't acknowledge how bad her situation is and how hopeless she feels.

They must begin to acknowledge it. They must face the fact that progressive torture is happening here, in America, in the 1990s, to a woman they know.

And even though she may not be able to ask for it, she needs all the help she can get.

3

Life Doesn't Have to Be Like This

HOW TO SPOT A BATTERER BEFORE AN ABUSIVE RELATIONSHIP BEGINS

Profile of a Batterer

An abusive man may exhibit only a few of the following qualities early in a relationship. More and more of them will appear as the relationship progresses. Every woman and girl should be familiar with the following profile. If she is involved with a batterer, she will recognize him. If not, she should take note so that if a new man in her life begins displaying these qualities, she will know what he is, what he is doing, and what he wants to do to her life.

1. Inability to Function Emotionally
Is he unable to discuss his emotions openly?

Does he have difficulty in discussing any problems calmly and rationally?

How does he deal with stress? Is he calm and reasonable or is he given to outbursts of violent behavior such as swearing, throwing things, breaking windows, kicking doors?

2. His Attitudes Toward Women
Does he think women are inferior to men? Does he frequently mention this perceived inferiority?

Does he make derisive comments about women drivers, "women's libbers," or dumb women? Has he resisted her suggestion that such comments are out-of-date or insulting?

Does he frequently use demeaning terms such as "broads," "chicks," "gals," or "babes" when speaking about women?

Does he refuse to consider women as equals?

Does he believe that women should be "submissive," "quiet," "dependent," "respectful," or "know their place?"

Does he feel strongly about the relative positions of men and women?

In the family?

In the home?

In religious life?

In the work place?

Does he resent the idea of working for a woman?

3. His Childhood Recollections

Did he come from an abusive home where he saw his mother or sisters beaten or severely dominated by his father?

Was he a battered or abused child?

Does something in his life, such as the lack of a good education, the lack of marketable skills, the lack of friends and permanent relationships, the inability to get and keep a job, or early family problems cause him to suffer from low self-esteem?

Does he have a habit of blaming others for what he does or for what happens to him?

4. Alcohol or Drug Abuse

Does he have a problem with alcohol or drugs? Does he drink too much or use illegal drugs?

Does he refuse to admit that he has a problem?

Does he insist that he is only a social drinker or a social drug user?

Does he say things like, "I can stop anytime I want to?"

Does he ignore all requests to temper or moderate his behavior?

Has he ever humiliated her for her opinions about his behavior?

Does he insist, often forcibly, that she join him in his bouts of drinking or drug abuse?

Has he ever slipped alcohol or drugs into her food or beverages?

Has he ever become irrational when he has been drinking or taking drugs?

Has he ever shouted or sworn at her when he was drinking or taking drugs?

Has he ever shoved her or slapped her when he was drinking or taking drugs?

5. Criticism and Suppression

Is he constantly critical of her? Does he belittle everything she says and does?

Does he constantly say negative things about her?

Does he deride her opinions?

Does he try to make her feel stupid, ignorant, or incompetent? Does he tell her that she is stupid or that she can't do anything right?

Does he make jokes at her expense in the presence of others?

Does he demean her hopes? Dreams? Aspirations? Ambitions?

Does he make her question her own abilities?

Does he resent any interest she has in furthering her education? Does he say things like, "A woman doesn't need to go to school to learn how to push a baby buggy?"

Does he say negative things about her friends or her family?

Does he make her feel that she is not competent enough to get along in the world without his help and direction?

6. Isolation

Does he "love her so much" that he cannot bear for her to be in the company of anyone else?

Her family?

Old friends?

Even female friends?

Does he tell her that he suffers when he sees her talking to anyone else?

Is he unhappy, moody, or disagreeable when she spends time alone with her friends or family?

Does he forbid her to spend time alone with her friends or family?

Is he so interested in every aspect of her daily life that he refuses to allow her to have even a casual telephone conversation without listening in?

Does he refuse to permit her to leave home alone, even to go to work?

Has he suggested moving away from the community in which her friends or family members live (for reasons of business, a promotion, security, or "privacy")?

Has he suggested moving to an isolated location such as a lake cottage, mountain retreat, or rural area?

Does he refuse to let her associate with her old friends, business colleagues, or co-workers, or to have friends outside their marriage or relationship?

Does he insist on picking up all the mail, then censor it before she sees it?

Is she forbidden to seek medical attention?

7. Jealousy

Is he so jealous that he becomes suspicious of her every action?

Is he so possessive that he wants to dictate her every move?

Does he accuse her of doing things she never even thought of doing?

Does he accuse her of trying to attract other men by her walk?

Her choice of clothing?

Her way of talking?

Her hairstyle or makeup?

Her actions?

If she is permitted to keep her job, does he accuse her of having affairs with men at work?

If she has no job, does he accuse her of having affairs with strange men or men she knows casually while he is away at work?

Has he threatened to confront men she knows casually and accuse them of being her lovers?

Is he jealous of her female friends as well?

8. Control

Does he try to control every aspect of her life?

Does he refuse to understand that she is a capable, competent, adult?

Does he refuse to understand her need to be treated with respect?

Does she have to ask his permission before doing even ordinary things?

Going anywhere or visiting anyone?

Having guests visit her home when he is at home?

Having guests visit her home when he is away?

Making telephone calls?

Writing personal checks?

Shopping for food or clothing?

Handling money of any amount for any reason?

Attending the religious service of her choice?

9. Insecurity

Does her partner seem to switch from the loving Dr. Jekyll or the hateful Mr. Hyde with little or no warning?

Does she worry about who will walk through the door when he comes home — the Dr. Jekyll she loves or the Mr. Hyde she fears?

Does she find that she is constantly walking on eggs because she never knows what he will say or do next?

Does he respond irrationally to rational situations or conversations?

Does he fly into a rage for no apparent reason?

Is she constantly afraid that he will become violent?

Does he refuse to believe that he should suffer any consequences for his violent behavior?

Does he blame her, and not himself, for his violent behavior?

10. Perfectionism

Does she find herself trying to be perfect?

To keep a perfect home?

To raise perfect children?

To keep the children silent at home when he is there?

To keep the children out of his way?

To serve perfect meals?

Is she willing to do *anything* to avoid a verbal or physical confrontation with him?

Does she have to lie to him in order to protect herself or her children from severe punishment for minor infractions of his rigid laws?

Does she feel that she is always fighting desperately to save the relationship?

Does she suspect that she is losing her own personality in this relationship?

11. Threats

Does he warn her that he is going to beat her? Verbal warnings about abuse should never be ignored.

When he warns her of a beating, does he insist that she do something to keep it from happening?

Does he threaten to harm her, her children, her parents, or other family members if she does not do what he wants?

Does he threaten to harm her, her children, her parents, or other family members if she tries to leave him?

Does he threaten to harm her, her children, her parents, or other family members if she tells anyone about his violence against her?

Does he threaten to harm her, her children, her parents, or other family members if she seeks medical treatment for the wounds he has inflicted on her?

Has he ever threatened her with a weapon?

Has he ever said he will kill her?

12. Punishment

Does he believe that a man has the right to physically discipline or punish his partner?

Does he tell her that God made man superior to woman and thereby gave him the privilege of beating her?

Does he tell her that he batters her as punishment for her misbehavior?

Does he tell her that the abuse she receives is all her fault?

Does he say that he would rather not abuse her but that she is forcing him to do so?

Does he tell her that he batters her to teach her to become a better person?

Does he tell her that he is doing this for her own good?

13. Physical Abuse

Has she ever found herself making excuses to friends, family, co-workers, neighbors, or others about her bumps, black and blue marks, headaches, painful walking, limp, or otherwise abused appearance?

Has he ever shoved her?
Knocked her down?
Slapped her?
Punched her?
Kicked her?
Hit her in the stomach?
Bitten her?
Blackened her eye?
Hit her hard enough to open a bleeding wound?
Caused bruises?
Raised welts?
Broken her tooth?
Broken her bone?
Pushed her down the stairs?
Attempted to shoot her?
Attempted to strangle her?
Attempted to suffocate her?
Attempted to stab her?

Does she tell herself that each level of abuse is not all that bad, but that if he ever did anything more she would leave?

Has the level of physical abuse escalated to the point at which she suspects she could be seriously injured, maimed, or even killed?

Is she afraid to leave?

Is she afraid to stay?

Forewarned is Forearmed

Demonstrating just one or two of these characteristics does not automatically make a man a batterer; not every man who has ever made a disparaging remark about women drivers is beating his wife or girlfriend. But there are striking similarities among men who abuse women, and all women should learn to recognize a potential batterer before it is too late.

The following stories show how similar to one another batterers really are.

Part Two

FOUR BATTERED WOMEN

and Their Stories

4

Courtenay

THE LUCKIEST GIRL IN THE WORLD

Courtenay is a strikingly pretty young woman with ivory skin and sparkling eyes. Her long legs and classic features bring to mind the easy grace and unpracticed elegance of the young Katherine Hepburn. She is a daughter of the Old South, accustomed to all the rights and privileges such upper-class rank bestows. She is well educated, well traveled, intelligent, creative, chic, and charming. The world ought to be Courtenay's oyster. But this beautiful young woman has attempted suicide.

Why?

His name is Pete.

I started dating Pete at the end of my junior year in high school. My friend Melanie had a crush on him. She went on and on about him and insisted that I have a look at him. I thought he was really nice, and since he hadn't paid any attention to Melanie, I felt that he was fair game. It wasn't long before I was dating him. That was my first mistake.

Pete was always a lot of fun and I got along with him better than with anybody else I've ever gone out with . . . ever! We would go for long walks and talk and talk for hours. He told me that we had been a lot alike as children. He had even made the same kind of bizarre airplane models and he had even painted big teeth on them just as I had. He was creative. He was interested in writing and art. He seemed to be interested in everything I was interested in.

I'm convinced that, at first, the problems Pete and I had were my fault. Toward the end of my senior year I started noticing other attractive boys and thinking I might like to go out with them. I didn't tell Pete about it because I didn't think I needed to. After all, we weren't married, and I was free to date whomever I pleased. But I never did anything I thought would really hurt him. Strangely, while I was dating other boys, I was accusing him of dating other girls. So you see, I was a real rat!

Meanwhile, Melanie started spreading rumors. I attended a deb ball in New York with one of the local boys and Melanie told Pete we were having an illicit affair. Of course that upset him. He was violently angry, but I was able to calm him that time. The next time I was not as successful.

The first I saw of what I can only call his verbal violence happened shortly after my daddy died. The incident involved a boy named Jodie in whom I had never had any romantic interest at all. But Jodie is a terrific racquetball player, and I enjoyed playing racquetball with him. Pete didn't play. I realized that he would be very jealous if he suspected I was with Jodie. Pete made me feel squeamish about everything I did and everyone I saw. I couldn't see any reason to give up playing because Pete didn't play and I didn't want him to be jealous, so I told him I was playing with another girl. Pete called her to check up on me and found that she had been at home all afternoon. He called me in a rage. When I admitted I had played racquetball with Jodie, it made him even more furious.

That evening he came peeling into the driveway. I ran up to his car, and he lurched it forward so that I would have to back off. He said a lot of bad things about me, really terrible things that were incoherent and horrible, calling me the worst names you can imagine and using the most awful language. He said all of our disagreements and all of our fights were my fault. Finally he said, "I just want to tell you one thing." He was talking in a low, angry voice I had never heard before and I couldn't hear the rest of the sentence. I thought I heard him say, "I don't ever want to see you again." I called out "Wait! What did you say? I couldn't hear you." But he just drove off, very angry, very ugly.

I came into the house, feeling terrible about myself, all torn up and dramatic as only a high school senior can be. I threw myself down on the floor. I had dealt with so much when my daddy died, I felt as though I didn't have the courage to deal with anything anymore. I was so unhappy about myself that I thought I couldn't go on. I grabbed a bottle of prescription pills and started chewing them.

Fortunately, my mother found me and put me to bed. I didn't do that simply because I was unhappy. It wasn't just that he said he didn't want to see me again. It was something more. He was so different, it was like he wasn't even the same person. He was so angry, I couldn't believe it. His anger didn't seem to show any sign of relief. In a way it was boundless.

And I felt that it was all my fault. I felt as though I had done that to him.

All this upset my older brother enough that he called Pete and threatened him with serious consequences if he didn't come back and apologize to me. Evidently, Pete can be easily intimidated by large men who are stronger than he is, because he came right over to apologize. This was when I began to see what he was really made of. I thought he was apologizing because he found out what I had tried to do and he felt so awful about having done that to me. But as it turned out, he wasn't apologizing because he was concerned for me. He was apologizing because he didn't want to be blamed if anything happened to me. Still, he was so much fun to be with and he could be so charming that I continued to go out with him.

My mother and I had planned a trip overseas during that next summer, and we invited him to travel with us. During that trip, we were both able to see how uptight, how jealous, and how really strange he was. He was jealous about things other than simply interference from other men. He was jealous about experiences. When we went to St. Peter's Basilica in Rome, he wouldn't even go inside. He didn't want to see the Basilica. He wanted to go to the souvenir shop across the street and buy postcards of it to show the people back home. He never went in anywhere to experience anything.

Of course we knew from the beginning that he had never been

abroad and that we would have to downplay the fact that we had been to these places before. We knew how much he hated the idea that my parents had given me the opportunity to travel and his hadn't been able to give him the same opportunity. So Mother and I found ourselves having to be careful about everything we said or did.

Even so, there were times when we couldn't contain ourselves. I loved the Vatican! The art and the architecture are glorious! He had come all that way, but he didn't even make it to the door of the Sistine Chapel, the Library, or the Basilica. I wanted to go inside, but I didn't want to hurt his feelings. He was so strong in his refusal that I didn't want to abandon him. I decided that since we would be in Rome for several days I would find time to go back later on. Of course I never did. Somehow, without really saying anything, he had managed to prevent me from doing what I wanted to do.

The same thing happened at Cambridge University in England. It was the weirdest thing! He spent the whole day speaking with a British accent and acting as though he were a Cambridge student, but when we finally got to the school he refused to walk onto the campus. I guess he didn't want to see what he couldn't be part of. Perhaps he was afraid to see that the students were wealthier and more "British" than he was, which is peculiar because he's not British at all; his family is Hungarian.

By that time, Mother and I were both onto his little game. I was determined not to miss out on anything else that I wanted to do, so we left him at a hardware store just off the campus. He was waiting for us when we came out and he took great pleasure in telling us how an American student at Cambridge had asked him for directions and how he had put on his best British accent and convinced the student that he was a native.

I can't explain it, but he seemed to have a real desire not to listen to anybody. He hated to face anyone who was smarter or richer or more handsome or he thought was in any way better. Even though he may have wanted to be part of things, he denied their validity by refusing to be part of them.

The last straw was when we went to visit the British riding academy which I had attended. I wanted to see it so badly that I couldn't contain my enthusiasm. It was wonderful to be back at this place where happy memories were just everywhere for me. I had been so happy there when Daddy was still alive and our family was all together. Everything was wonderful back then. My horse, Moonglow, was still there and I wanted to see him. Mother took pictures of us, of the horse and me, of me and the horse, and then pictures of the horse and me again. After a while, we turned around and realized that Pete had left. Since he wasn't the center of attention he had gone out to sit and sulk in the car. This time, he was jealous of the horse!

He was on unfamiliar turf. He had never had an opportunity to do anything like that. He was unhappy with me for enjoying myself so much, and he tried to make me feel guilty. It was a great experience for me to be back there, and I wasn't going to give it up without a good reason. But he made me feel that I was a fool. He said I was acting stupid and childish to be so excited about a horse. Even though he knew how much I loved it, he always tried to make me feel that riding was a very pretentious thing to do.

I guess you could interpret his actions to mean he felt threatened, but he had a way of really spoiling things for me. When he didn't like something, or when he wasn't interested in something, or when he wasn't the center of attention, he would do his best to make me feel bad about it. He questioned my motives or said I did things because I was pretentious. His reasons for doing things were always pure and wise, without any blemish. But the truth was that a lot of things he did were purely for effect. And a lot of the people he saw to get into their good graces. He gloried in his "networking" abilities and his abilities to find people he could use.

Pete kept borrowing money during the trip. Money became a big issue with him, but Mom didn't really care. She would loan him money, and she would pay for a lot of things without ever being asked or expecting to be paid back. We were on the trip together and she treated him as though he was just another one of her kids. She would simply give him the money. All he had to pay for was his plane ticket. She paid for his meals, hotels, and everything else.

It got to the point, though, where she started to wonder what he was doing with all the money she was giving him. Then we had an incident over money that was a real eye-opener. By this time we had agreed that we could all go off on our own and do what we were interested in doing without having to be constantly together.

I guess it must have been in Milan that he asked for money and mom gave him about $20 in Lire so that he could pay for a bite to eat and visit some museums. When he came back, we discovered that he hadn't gone to see anything at all but he had bought himself a silk shirt. That wasn't why she had given him the money. For some reason that seemed like a really nasty thing for him to do. We started to think he was doing this to see how far he could push us.

There were some nice times, but things got very warped during that trip. I began to feel as though I had to be the referee between Pete and my mom. She's a pretty strong personality who can be pushed only so far, and he was pushing as hard as he could. I was afraid that he would push so far that she would start pushing back and that would not be pleasant. I was beginning to resent him for trying so hard to make it difficult for us. By the time we got back to the States, I had decided that our relationship was over. I thought he had a really evil, warped, mean, petty side. It was as though he couldn't feel good about himself unless he made everybody else feel bad about themselves.

After we were home for a while, tensions relaxed and everything was fine, except that I don't think I saw him quite as much as I had in the past. We went to separate colleges. He would drive over to visit me on Sundays, and our Sundays together were simply fantastic. He was always great fun when he could control where we went and what we did. I truly looked forward to seeing him. We went along like that for a while and I began to think that maybe I had been wrong about him.

As the year progressed, I realized that the most important courses I needed to take were given at my state university or at Harvard and I would have to go to one place or the other. He encouraged me to come to the university. He even came to serenade under my window at night and whisper "not Boston ... not Boston . . ." Finally, I decided to transfer to the university. My decision wasn't made exclusively because he was there, but I must admit that that could have been a large part of it.

When he heard that I was transferring to the university, he started to change. He started calling everybody "dude" and wearing exotic clothes that gave him that suntanned, surfer look. When I finally got to the university, he didn't want anything to do with me. He acted as though I wasn't blonde enough or tanned enough for him anymore. He said the things we had once enjoyed so much were boring and simple. He knew how much he was hurting my feelings, but it didn't bother him at all. He was enjoying the opportunity to show me how much more important than me he was, that this was his turf, and that I didn't fit in. I decided he had turned into a monster, and I didn't want to see him anymore.

I started to date Cliff from time to time. Then one afternoon Pete asked me out to lunch. We had a surprisingly nice time, and we returned to my apartment to get a book I wanted to lend him. I walked into my apartment and, somehow, I realized that Cliff was there. My roommate must have let him in. I don't know how I knew he was there, I just sensed it. We walked into the kitchen and all of a sudden, Cliff jumped out from behind the refrigerator! Pete acted as though I had done something terrible. He said something really nasty, and he turned around and left. When I called him later, I discovered that he thought I had planned the whole thing to humiliate him. It was awful!

We didn't see each other for months after that. I started seeing Cliff regularly, and Pete started seeing someone else. One day he called and said that after all we had meant to each other in the past he thought we ought to be friends. We decided we could go out for lunch and just be friends, or as close to friends as you can be with anyone you had been in love with for that long. So we went out to lunch. It was all very pleasant, and we decided we would see each other every now and then, simply as friends.

This was when the really bad stuff happened.

About that time, I was working on a major project for my most important class. It included a series of graphs and charts along with the written material. It was the last night to get the work done.

I had borrowed a typewriter to finish the written material, but when I started to type the final draft I realized that what I had borrowed was a dot matrix typewriter. That's the kind of typewriter that makes the typing look as though it had been done on a computer. I knew Pete owned a regular typewriter, so I called and asked if he would let me come to his place and finish my paper. He said sure.

I packed all my stuff together and, since my car was in the shop, I took the bus to his place. Time was getting tight. I had wasted much of my scheduled time fooling with the dot matrix typewriter and I still needed to do some touch-up work on the charts and graphs. I was doing the touch-up work when Pete volunteered to type the final draft of my written material. He always made me feel as though he was smarter and more capable of doing everything and anything, so even though he was typing basically what I had written, he would ask if we could change this paragraph or that phrase to "make it better." We would discuss it and then he would type it. We finally finished the work at about 1:30 in the morning. Since I had no car and the buses were no longer running, Pete drove me home. When we got to my apartment, we had another surprise. You can guess who my roommate had let in!

The only reason Cliff was at my apartment at that hour was that he was dropping off some mounting boards which I needed to use for my charts. He was reaching for the doorknob, ready to leave, when I came bursting through the door. It was completely innocent, but it was the worst case of bad timing you could imagine. Pete didn't say anything ugly that time. He just got that awful expression on his face and ran down the stairs.

I said, "Oh no!" and Cliff could see how upset I was, so he stayed and talked to me for a while.

Then, just about the time Pete got home, my phone rang. It was Pete, and he was really angry. He demanded to know what Cliff was doing at my apartment at that hour of the night. He began calling me horrible names, and saying the most awful things about me. He was swearing, lying, and being really abusive. He was using the same awful language and that same awful voice he used that time in my driveway. Finally, he became so ugly that I hung up the phone.

Cliff was still there, and he was wondering what was going on. It was his turn to ask questions. He wanted to know what I'd been doing at Pete's apartment at that hour of the morning. But the difference between them was that Cliff was willing to believe me when I told him I had been working on my project.

Pete called back. I said I had work to do and hung up again.

He called back immediately, still angry and incoherent. He said, "You'd better not use any of that stuff I helped you with."

I said, "Don't do this to me. I have six hours to get this project turned in. I don't have time for this ugliness."

He said, "So help me God, you'd better not use it. I'm going

to find out if you do and you'll be sorry. You'd better not use it."
He was seriously threatening me.

I said, "I've got to use it. I don't have time to do it all over
again."

Pete kept calling me. I kept hanging up, and he kept calling
and calling for over an hour. He was saying some strange things. I
mean, some really bizarre things. I finally said "All right. I have
no choice. I'm going to re-do the project the way I had it in the
first place."

He kept calling until I disconnected the phone, but as soon as
I did, the phone began to ring in my roommate's room. She wasn't
getting too much sleep anyway. I finally talked to Pete on her
phone and I told him I wasn't going to use the stuff he had typed.

Cliff realized that I was dreadfully pressed for time so he
decided he would stay and do all the mounting while I retyped the
fifteen pages of the paper. We stayed up and worked all night until
we got the thing finished. Cliff finally left at six so that he could go
study for his own exams. I put everything together, ready to get it
all turned in by eight o'clock.

I was exhausted. I'd had no sleep. A friend and I decided to go
get a cup of coffee while the instructor was judging the projects.
We were walking along to the coffee shop and I saw Pete coming
directly toward us. I said "Hi," as though nothing had happened.
He said nothing, but we realized that he had turned around and
was following us down the sidewalk. Before I knew what had
happened, Pete had come up behind me, grabbed me by the neck,
and started strangling me. It was in the morning, in the middle of
the public sidewalk, and here I was being strangled. I couldn't
catch my breath. It was horrible! I tried to get away from him but I
couldn't. I knew I had to do something, so I reached back and
grabbed him and threw him against a wall. It kind of knocked the
wind out of him but he got up and ran off.

My friend said, "My God, who is that? Do you know him? Is
he drunk? Is he crazy?"

I said, "Well, he's kind of an old boyfriend."

My friend was in shock and so was I. I just thought Pete had
finally lost it. I felt good about breaking off any kind of contact
with him whatsoever.

We went back to the school, and I found out that my project
had done so well that I was one of a group of seven top students

who were eligible for a scholarship.

When they posted the list that afternoon, I went to look at it, sort of to glory in seeing my name among the top seven. But it wasn't there. It wasn't anywhere on the list! I went to see the instructor to ask why my name was left off the list. She was rather evasive.

Do you want to tell me anything about your project?" she asked.

I said no, there wasn't anything to tell her. Then I asked why she had asked me that.

"Well," she said, "a fellow named "Mike" came by my office and told me that you had plagiarized the entire project."

She didn't say whether my project was supposed to have been copied or anything. She only said that it was plagiarized. I had difficulty in convincing the instructor that this wasn't true. I reminded her that she herself had seen me working on all my charts and graphs during class. She had even helped me with my ideas in formulating the written material. There was no way the project could have been plagiarized. I couldn't believe the instructor would take the word of a stranger who had walked in off the street over that of a student she had known all year. I couldn't believe that I had been so close to what I wanted, had had it in my hand, and it was going to be taken away from me! I kept thinking it was a bad dream.

I called Pete and asked if "Mike" was there.

He said, "There's no Mike at this number. What are you talking about?"

I said, "You know exactly what I'm talking about."

He denied it! He knew that I'd found him out, and he denied it!

Finally, he said, "I told them I helped you type it. I didn't say you had done anything wrong." When he said that, I asked if he would go back to my instructor and tell her what he had just told me. I had to be very nice to him because I knew he was crazy, but I needed him to clear this mess up. But he wouldn't do it. He absolutely refused to do it.

I was terribly upset, and I called my mom and told her what had happened. By this time, Mother was no longer willing to put up with any more problems either from Pete or from the university, so she got into her car and drove directly down to the university. Six hours later she was sitting in the president's office, demanding a conference with the chairman of the department as well as with my instructor. I don't know how she did it, but she's a formidable lady and somehow she was able to get the whole thing straightened out so that I didn't have to lose everything I had earned.

Of course, I was determined never to see Pete again. But I seemed to have a lot of strange troubles at the university that following semester. I was constantly getting phone calls in which the other party would hang up as soon as I answered. This happened at every hour of the day or night and it began to be rather frightening.

My car had an unusual number of flat tires. Sometimes the air was simply let out of the tires, and sometimes they were puncture flats that could be fixed. But they seemed to happen with an alarming regularity. It didn't enter my head that someone could intentionally be puncturing my tires. Then one night, as Cliff and I were leaving the little fashion boutique where I worked, Cliff suddenly started running as fast as he could. There's a kind of high fence that runs along the side of the boutique, and Cliff took off running around that fence. When he came back, he said, "Well, I've just chased down your old boyfriend."

"What?"

"Pete's been watching us over that fence." Cliff said. He chased him, but he couldn't quite catch up with him.

I didn't hear from Pete for quite a long time after that, but I felt awful that I had gone with him for so long and that it had turned out so badly. I felt that somehow it was my fault that it turned out the way it had. I hated to think that someone I once cared so much about now hated me.

And then one day I received an envelope with my address typed on the outside. There was no return address and all the envelope contained was a couple of photo booth pictures Pete and I had taken on our second date back in high school. I thought I had lost these pictures, but it was so sweet to have them again. It was so romantic!

Still, I didn't call Pete for months and months. After a while, when I finally broke up with Cliff, I was feeling so blue that I broke down and called Pete. He was warm and wonderful like his old self. He said he'd wondered if I were ever going to call him again. We got together that evening and had a really nice dinner. I didn't feel threatened dating a man who once attempted to strangle me because I knew him so well and he was acting like himself, like he used to act when we were back in high school. Besides, I didn't ever let myself act weak around him or let him think he could control me. I've seen him since then, but I didn't ever get close enough to let him blow up in my face again. I kept thinking that maybe he would apologize and everything would go back to being as nice as it once was.

My older brother found out that I'd been seeing Pete again, and he wasn't at all pleased. He called Pete and told him exactly what would happen to him if he ever tried to contact me by phone, mail, or anything. Now, we already know that Pete is easily intimidated by large men who are stronger than he is, and my brother had gotten even larger and stronger than when I was in high school. I believe he had also gotten a bit more forceful in what he had to say to Pete.

Naturally, I was furious with my brother! I'm not a child. I was humiliated and hurt to think that my own brother would do a thing like that to me. But my brother had really put the fear into Pete and he absolutely would not have anything to do with me after that.

It took me a while to get over my fascination with Pete, but now that I can look back at the situation, I realize it was like the fascination a small child has with a snake. It can charm you, but it can kill you. I can recognize all the terrible things he did to me. And worse, I can recognize the terrible things he could have done to me if I had continued to see him. Pete's a pretty dangerous person, and I am thankful that my family loved me enough to stand by me and stand up for me until I could see it for myself. I escaped a lot of suffering and pain. I must be the luckiest girl in the world.

What Happened

Courtenay graduated from the university and is successful in her chosen field. She knows that she was rescued from a potentially disastrous situation and is now extremely careful about relationships. She is one of the lucky ones. Pete's next girlfriend may not be so lucky.

5

Lorraine

THE HIGH PRICE OF FIGHTING BACK

Lorraine looks as fragile as a porcelain doll with large, round eyes and tiny hands. Her delicate features and gentle ways make her look exactly like a cheerful, young mother one might meet at PTA meetings or in the Junior League. Lorraine's story is horrifying, but it is important because it shows what can happen to a battered woman who has remained in the battering situation so long that her life has veered out of control.

Her friends and family thought Lorraine had it all. She lived in a large, attractive home in the suburbs. She had two beautiful children who were quiet and well-mannered and a strikingly handsome husband whose dedication to his church activities seemed admirable to a fault. Everyone who knew Lorraine was astonished to learn the truth about her life.

By that time it was too late.

Lorraine was in prison.

Things might have been different if I had been able to ask someone for help. I might have been able to make a better life for myself and my children. Christopher might have gone into some kind of therapy to help him control his violent behavior toward me. We might have been able to turn our lives around. But it's too late now, and I will never know if I could have made a difference. I didn't know how to tell anyone what was happening to me. I don't know if anyone would have believed me because I could hardly believe it myself. I didn't know who to talk to. It wasn't exactly the sort of thing you want to tell your parents. At first I considered the experiences I was having a nightmare and later I simply felt depraved. What I kept hidden is still painful and hard for me to speak about.

I loved Christopher when we got married and I thought he would be the most wonderful husband in the world. He was so handsome and so dependable. I thought he was the most dependable person I had ever met. He was always well-dressed and he had such elegant manners. He would open doors for me and hold my chair out and help me on with my coat. He was thoughtful and concerned about everything I did, everyone I saw, and every place I went. I thought he really cared about all the little things that were happening in my life. It never occurred to me that he asked all those questions because he wanted to check up on me or because he wanted to control every move I made.

After we got married, he started working on my mind. He began to be physically and mentally abusive. He found ways to tell me I was stupid and ugly. No matter how I dressed or what I did, no matter how hard I tried, I couldn't change his opinion of me. He said so many awful things I finally began to believe them myself. He hit me in the stomach when I became pregnant, and pushed me down the stairs. I can only thank God that somehow neither of my babies was injured.

I suffered so much, but I was ashamed to tell anybody about it. I had never heard of this happening to anyone I knew and I thought I had done something terrible to deserve such treatment. I thought the abuse couldn't be any worse. But I was wrong. It got a lot worse after each of our babies was born. I never knew what might cause him to fly into a rage. He would beat me for any reason and for no reason at all. Anything could get him started. He would beat me if dinner was a little late or if it was a few minutes early. He would hit me if the babies were crying, if the telephone was ringing, if the window was open, or if the window was shut.

Christopher was abnormally jealous of our little girls and everything they did made him angry. Babies cry. It's something babies do, but the sound of the babies crying drove Christopher crazy. I was afraid he would turn on them and hurt them or even kill them. Somehow, when he started to hit me I always found a way to lead him away from their room and away from them. Two or three times, he beat me until I was unconscious. I always wore long sleeves and long pants to cover the bruises. I lied about the bruises I couldn't hide and told people I had fallen or bumped into something.

I keep asking myself why I didn't run away. Why didn't I leave him? The truth is, I was terrified of him. Christopher had started to threaten me. Before long, he found a way to threaten me every day. He said he would take my babies away if I ever told anyone what he did to me, or if I ever tried to leave him. He told me I would never see my little girls alive again. He said that they would "just disappear."

As if this weren't bad enough, Christopher became involved in religion. He told me he had "found God" and "found a church home." That sounded so good to me! I hoped and prayed that the Lord would enter his heart and help him change his ways. But I soon learned that he wasn't interested in the normal kind of religion I had always known and loved. He wasn't involved with a normal church where they had stained glass windows, a choir and Sunday School, Bible study classes, and a normal pastor. He was involved in some kind of charismatic church where they spent their time speaking in tongues, doing exorcisms, and "casting out demons." It wasn't long before his religion became an obsession, and his obsession quickly began to involve me.

That was when he began to sexually abuse me. I can't tell you all the horrible and painful things he did to me because they are perverted and sick. I was always suffering with internal infections but he wouldn't let me go to the doctor for help because he was afraid I would tell the doctor what was happening.

He told me that God had decreed that he should do these things to me. He somehow convinced me I would be cursed if I didn't let him do all the shameful things his God had told him to do to me. He began to tell me I was possessed and that it wasn't God but Satan who was making him do all these horrible things to me. And of course, he said Satan had nothing to do with him or his actions. He said Satan was in me! My life was so horrible I began to wish that I could die. I began to think that maybe I *was* possessed. I began doubting my own mind and wondering if Satan really was in me.

After about six months of the worst kind of torture, Christopher told me he was going to "triumph over Satan." He said he was going to have it "over and done with." He was going to "get Satan out of me for good." He came after me and I knew that this would be more than a beating. I knew he meant to kill me.

I couldn't just let him kill me. I couldn't! I realized that in all these years I had never once even tried to fight back. This was the first time I had ever tried to protect myself and I was terrified. I ran to where he kept his hunting rifle and I loaded it.

Christopher was a big man. He grabbed the barrel of the gun and began to pull it away from me. I fought to keep it because I knew that if he got it he would kill me with it. While we were struggling, the gun went off.

All I can remember was crying, begging someone, anyone, to help me. I don't remember much about what else happened that terrible night. My neighbors must have heard the noise and called the police. I didn't think about calling the police. I had called them once when Christoper first started to beat me. I had asked them to help me, and I tried to report the abuse, but the policeman I spoke with only told me to "behave myself" and "not to do things to make my husband angry."

Someone took my babies and me out of the house. I didn't even realize that Christopher was dead until after the police detective finally told me they were charging me with murder.

They took me down to the jail and set my bail. My brother had to sell his car to get me out of prison. My attorney hired a psychiatrist who said I was suffering from the Battered Woman Syndrome. I had never heard of such a thing. I was indicted for murder, aggravated manslaughter, manslaughter in the heat of passion, and manslaughter and possession of a weapon for illegal purposes.

I didn't do any of those things. I didn't have a weapon for illegal purposes. I didn't own a weapon at all. I don't know anything about guns. It was Christopher's hunting rifle and that was the first time I had ever put my hands on it. All I did was fight for my life. I know that if I had not fought back that one time, Christoper would have killed me. I'm not even sure it's my fault Christopher is dead. He could have pulled the trigger himself during the scuffle when he was grabbing at me, trying to pull the gun away from me.

I'll never know.

I have lost my freedom. My friends and relatives think I'm a murderer. Worst of all, I am separated from my children, and I can never watch them grow up. I know that little girls need their mother, but I'm a stranger to them. One day, when they are old enough to ask questions, I will have to find a way to tell them what happened between their parents on that terrible night. I have lost any chance I will ever have in life, but I suffer worse for my children than I do for myself. How can they hold their heads up in the world when everyone around them knows what kind of family they come from?

What Happened

Lorraine was sentenced to prison. Fortunately, her brother is willing and able to bring up her children in her absence. Because she fought to defend herself, Lorraine has forfeited any opportunity she might have had to lead a normal life.

6

Casey

THIS NIGHTMARE CAN'T BE HAPPENING TO ME!

Casey's story shows that battering can happen to any woman, regardless of how smart or successful she is. At thirty-five, Casey was chic, sophisticated, and at the top of the career ladder, the undisputed national leader in her field. She dressed in designer suits and drove the latest BMW equipped with a state-of-the-art cellular phone. She paid cash for her condominium at the most prestigious address in the city and filled it with palace-size, oriental rugs, priceless antique furniture, and the finest of fine art.

Casey had it all.

Then she met Gunter, and the handsome, charming European swept her off her feet. She saw their whirlwind romance as a fairy tale relationship in which they were partners in everything: aspirations, romance, and business ventures combined. All of these things were at Casey's expense, of course. Gunter's finances were "temporarily in distress." This idyllic romance left Casey out of luck, out of work, abandoned, and broke.

I felt as though I had truly found my soul mate. At first, there was this overwhelming trust and the feeling that we could share everything. Everything! We could tell one another anything with absolute confidence.

I was swept away by the one true love I had ever experienced. I was completely giddy and just a little bit silly for someone as serious as I had always been. It was quite a heady experience. Gunter knew exactly the right things to say and do, exactly how I would react. It was nearly perfect. I felt I was walking on clouds. The only difficulty I could find in our relationship was that Gunter loved me so much he simply could not bear for us to be apart. There was nothing for me to do but to cut down on my out-of-town business trips.

I believed Gunter and I did everything in harmony. I had some serious reservations when he came up with a proposal for me to invest heavily in a favorite project of his. But I didn't see how I could refuse to go into it without hurting his feelings. I thought European men were so sensitive!

It was so delightful, so different for me to be dominated. And I thought I loved it. Although I was putting up all the money for that deal, Gunter insisted the whole thing be completely in his name. He told me that since we were dealing with Europeans, it would cause problems if it looked as if he were working for me. He said European men wouldn't accept a deal offered by a man who worked for a woman.

That struck me as odd. I knew it wasn't a smart business move but somehow I didn't really mind. By that time, we were engaged to be married, and I decided that after we married all our money would be combined anyhow, so it wouldn't matter in the long run.

Gunter was an incredibly charming man. I dated him for nine months and everything was lovely until our wedding night. Then he turned into another person. I should have had our marriage annulled immediately, but I had been in control of my life for so long, I couldn't believe this was happening to me. To *me!* There was a complete change in his personality. The Gunter I knew was gone, and I was married to a stranger, a totally different person.

There were no arguments or violence at first, just distance and indifference. And the demands. He demanded more and more financial commitment from me. I paid for everything, and everything was in his name. I even signed over my condo. I would do anything to please him.

We were only married for three months when I became

pregnant. It was quite accidental; we weren't trying to have a child, although I must admit that I wanted one. I wasn't a young girl anymore, and my biological clock was running overtime.

The first violence happened shortly after I told him I was pregnant. He hated the idea. He simply couldn't handle it. Without a word, he just lifted me up out of the bed and threw me down on the hardwood floor.

After that incident, nothing I said or did was ever right again. My hair was never right, my makeup was never right, my clothes were never right. He hated the sight of me in my maternity clothes and said I looked like a brood mare. He hit me for the slightest infraction or disagreement, or for not disagreeing with him. He hit me for anything and everything. He became angry over stupid things. All the discomforts of my pregnancy made it difficult enough for me to keep up my business affairs, but I was terrified that his beatings had done something to hurt or deform my baby.

Thank goodness, the baby was born healthy and normal. However, I had some serious complications with the birth, and I was forced to take a brief leave of absence from my business. When that happened, he told me I was now a "dressed-up and stupid housewife, no better than a cow." From that moment on, he said it was no longer worth his trouble to talk to me because he said I was too stupid to understand him.

I knew that many men have negative reactions to the birth of a first child. They are no longer the center of attention and they resent having to share the wife's attention with the baby. I believed I shouldn't spend all my time or give all my attention to my little newborn son, because my husband had to be treated like a little boy and pampered and petted as well. I tried to do that as best I could, but my health was poor. I was still weak, and it was very difficult.

One morning when I was changing the baby, Gunter seemed to go wild. Fortunately, he didn't attack me or the baby, but he started screaming and hitting his own head against the wall. I didn't know what was going on. Gunter is not an alcoholic and he doesn't take drugs, but he frightened me. I didn't know what to do. I felt as though the baby and I were in danger, so I took the baby and went to my parent's house. Once Gunter calmed down, he became his own charming self. He brought me flowers and candy; he apologized and promised never to let it happen again.

Then he came to take us away from the safety of my parents' home.

Shortly after that incident, he managed to find a significant business opportunity on the West Coast and it was only reasonable that our little family move out there so he could pursue it.

It was growing more and more difficult for me to continue my business and care for my baby. That move almost put me out of business, but I somehow managed to hang on. Once I reestablished myself on the West Coast, he found a reason why we had to move to the South. Then we moved back to the Coast. It seemed as though I was always moving, always being uprooted and separated from any friends I might make. I had a double reason for fighting tooth and nail to keep my business going. The only constant people in my life were my business associates.

The violence came and went whenever his fancy struck. One time I was talking with a client on the phone when Gunter suddenly took the heavy brass paperweight off my desk and broke my arm with it.

There were occasions when he would become so violent he would crack my head open. I've got a big scar on the back of my head where it had to be stitched together. I would call a cab and take my baby to the emergency room with me because I was afraid to leave him at home with his father. Although he had never attempted to harm our son, I never knew for sure that he wouldn't.

I would lie to the doctors about how my injuries had happened. I would say I had fallen and hurt myself or something of that nature. Gunter had somehow convinced me that I had to be careful of what I said about him because it would make him look bad in front of the business people he dealt with. I knew it would also have made me look stupid for allowing him to do these things to me. So I didn't dare admit to what was happening. Whenever I left the hospital, I would check into a motel and hide there for days until my husband calmed down.

He convinced me that everything that went wrong between us was my fault. He forced me to stand at attention for hours and repeat sentences after him, repeating the words exactly as he wanted me to say them, whether that was what I had intended to say or not. If I insisted on explaining my side of a story, he would listen to me very carefully but before I had finished what I had to say, I would pay the price for expressing my opinion. He tried to convince me that I was crazy.

I tried to love him. I tried to do everything I could do to make a happy marriage out of this situation, but I could never depend on him to have a reasonable reaction to an otherwise reasonable situation. His temper was horrible. If the sun came up in the morning, it might set him off. He would yank my arm and pull me up out of bed and knock me around the room. If the sun didn't come up in the morning, he might do the same thing. I had no control over my life.

He was a ruler once he got the upper hand. He thought he had all the answers. He had to be the supreme authority on any subject. He had to know it all. If anyone asked him the slightest question he would continue speaking for an hour or more, holding forth and lecturing about his own importance. He dominated any conversation he had. I was never allowed to say anything. More than that, no matter what was being discussed, he would insist that his "spiritual being" told him this or that. If I questioned him he would tell me he was involved with the "upper powers" which I could know nothing about.

He had rules and regulations about what I could and could not do. I was not allowed to lie down on the couch in the evening to watch television. It was my couch, which I had bought and paid for. He could lie down on it. I could not.

If it was eight o'clock at night and I wanted to take a shower, get into my gown and robe, and relax, I was not permitted to do so. I had to remain completely dressed in my business suit, hose, and heels all evening long. Showers were only to be taken before bedtime. Nightclothes were put on only moments before going to bed. He would not allow any music to be played while he was in the house. No radio, no record player, no music. I abided by his long list of rules and regulations so that he would not beat the hell out of me.

We had no friends and no social life, but he sometimes liked to entertain his clients with a barbecue at home. If he was barbecuing outdoors and brought something back to the table, he was the one who decided how everyone should want his or her meat cooked. If my steak was too rare and I wanted to put it back on the barbecue for a few minutes, it would put him into a rage. I learned to eat anything any way it was served—raw, rare, or burned to a crisp. I was simply not allowed to question anything. Anything could set him off. Anything. He used to weigh the hamburger patties on the postal scale. If one hamburger did not weigh exactly the same as the others he would go into a rage and take it out on me.

He didn't speak about moods; he spoke about "modes." No matter how hard or hectic my day might have been, I had to set the proper "mode" to encourage him to relax when he came home in the evening. If the "mode" wasn't right it was my fault, and I would suffer for it. I was his wife. His "mode" was my responsibility, and it was something else I couldn't do right.

He wanted to share me with other men. He believed in group sex and wanted me to become involved in exchange parties with different couples. I would refuse to do it, and he would beat me brutally. He wanted me to go to bed with men he had selected. Although I never did, he did everything possible to force me to do it. I was afraid to go to sleep at night because I feared I would be raped by the strange men he brought into our bedroom while I slept.

On the other hand, he forbade me to see men who had been lifelong friends. He even forbade me to see my women friends. If I was gone for more than an hour or two I was expected to call him and let him know where I was and what I was doing. He treated me as though he owned me.

He kept tabs on everything I did and every place I went. I couldn't even turn around in a restaurant or when we were walking down the street because he assumed I was looking at another man. I had to keep my eyes straight in front of me all the time.

I had to watch every word I said. If something struck him wrong, and if he decided I wasn't a "good girl" he would punish me by locking me in a closet for the whole day. This became a constant thing which, unfortunately, my son witnessed while he was growing up. Although the boy has never shown any signs of being troubled or abusive, I'm terrified that his father's behavior will have an effect on his life.

Being locked in the closet left me with serious claustrophobia. I'm terrified of any enclosed space, of riding in elevators or small cars. I can't stand to be in an airplane. This is a problem which has had considerable effect on my career because of the amount of traveling I am obliged to do. I can't drive on the freeway comfortably because I know that I might panic if I can't get off before the next exit. I can't drive downtown because I feel as though the tall buildings are closing in on me.

Sometimes we would go along for months without any violent incidents. Sometimes there would be a rash of violent arguments, and sometimes I would be battered continuously. There was a certain twisted expression that would come on his face. When I saw that expression, I knew he was going to beat me.

My husband had two distinct personalities: the handsome, sophisticated charmer and the brute who would beat me half to death. He had always maintained a very respectable place in the community. He could be an astute businessman and was well-respected, even something of an authority in his field. He was so handsome and charming that he had everyone in the business world convinced that he was successful. Even our neighbors believed he was a wonderful husband and devoted father. He was always impeccably dressed in the most expensive suits and shirts, and he had the most exquisite taste. We lived beautifully, even extravagantly, although this was because we were spending every penny of my income, which by this time was considerable.

Strange to say, it seemed as though the worse my family life became, the more my business thrived. My clients had become accustomed to looking for me in different cities. I could always make money for them, so they didn't mind waiting until I was settled in a new home or in a new town. More than that, the experience of knowing the various local markets firsthand gave me an insight I could never have acquired any other way.

In spite of this, Gunter was constantly telling me I could not survive without him. He convinced me that I could never do anything on my own. He would not allow me to make any decisions, not even the smallest decisions, because he said that I was not capable of making any responsible choices. I could never select a baby-sitter or pick the fabric for the draperies. In business, I was making multimillion-dollar deals, but at home I wasn't even permitted to decide which dress I would wear to an evening at the theater.

He would call me at work and threaten my secretary if she did not allow him to speak to me at once, no matter what I might be doing. He would interrupt important business meetings, conferences, and consultations to shout at me over the phone. I was only happy that he didn't show up at my office and humiliate me there.

If I was in a business meeting with him I was never allowed to talk. He would snap and snarl at me or tell me, "Shut up; you are only a stupid housewife." He would humiliate me publicly and tell me that I didn't know how to do anything but rinse diapers in a toilet and that I had no mind.

I heard it day after day until I believed it. In spite of all I had accomplished, in spite of my impressive income, in spite of my honors and awards, my self-esteem was destroyed. After my divorce, it took a long time before I could accept myself as a worthwhile person again.

I got the battering for breakfast, lunch, dinner, and midnight snack. I didn't know this could be happening to anyone else in the world, and I was ashamed. I came from a calm, typical American family. My father was not abusive. He was a decent family man who owned his own business and worked hard. My mother was a respectable housewife who kept an immaculate home, was a gourmet cook, the president of every women's volunteer society in town, and a wonderful mother. My parents worked out their problems together and raised all their children to be well-educated, hard working, responsible people. I had a good home life and a good family. I was never abused. I had never even heard about abuse.

Gunter came from the opposite kind of family. He had a weak, passive mother and an incredibly domineering father. In all the years we were married, his mother may have said as many as two sentences to me. She never talked. Although his father made a handsome living, his mother never seemed to have any comforts. She dressed in the cheapest housedresses and never went to a beauty shop or wore makeup. His father made all the decisions for their family without consulting her.

One reason I didn't leave Gunter was that I was terrified of him, terrified of myself, and terrified that I was inadequate. He always told me no other man would want my body because my breasts had started to sag and that "going to bed with me was like going to bed with two fried eggs." He told me I had a figure like a man.

I'm five feet and one inch tall, and my average weight is 104. I was having a lot of stomach trouble, and sometimes when I had stomach trouble or before a menstrual period, my stomach would bloat. It had nothing to do with fat; it had to do with water retention. He didn't care. He said my body humiliated him, and he demanded that I do strenuous exercises for hours at a time. He forced me to take strong dangerous medicines: diuretics, emetics, and laxatives. I didn't want to take them without a doctor's prescription, but I had no choice. I don't have a problem with my body. I never did. There's really nothing wrong with me, but he constantly drummed this into me until I believed it.

Sometimes he would hold his hands around my throat and choke me until I fainted. It was purely by accident that he never quite managed to murder me. The last time he became really violent, he tried to choke me. I was losing consciousness when, somehow, I decided I was not ready to die. I kicked him as hard as I could between his legs and ran out of the house. I ran down the streets of our neighborhood and managed to get away from him.

I knew this marriage wasn't right, but I didn't know what to do about it. I was separated from my friends and family. If my parents suspected what was happening, they were so far away that either they couldn't do anything, or they didn't know what to do to help me. I didn't dare discuss my problems with my business associates or I would lose all my accounts. I had to lie about my husband. If I said anything about the way he really was, it would have made him look bad and it would have made me look ridiculous. So I just kept quiet.

I developed terrible physical problems, stomach troubles, and digestive problems. I became depressed, and a physician recommended that I see a psychiatrist. Under the psychiatrist's advice, I admitted myself to a mental institution. I was diagnosed as having "extreme stress." I told Gunter it was because of my work, but it wasn't. It was because of him. I remained in the hospital for thirty days. Mostly, to "stay in reality," as my doctor would say, but also so that I wouldn't die. Under doctor's orders, I was to continue in out-patient therapy with the goal of making some significant decisions about what I was going to do with my life.

The week I came home, Gunter found a business opportunity in the Southwest and insisted that we move there immediately. Once again, I was uprooted. Not only was I separated from friends and family, but this time I was separated from the support I was now getting from my psychiatrist as well.

It was the nature of our individual businesses that both Gunter and I had to go on out-of-town business trips alone. In the course of Gunter's travels, it was necessary for him to be out late at night and to entertain at restaurants and nightclubs. One night, there was something different about him when he came home. He fell into bed but he left the contents of his pockets spread out on the dressing table. There was a receipt from a motel right down the street from where we lived. I found all sorts of evidence that he was having an affair with another woman and that this had been going on for some time. There were American Express receipts for motels in and around town, for restaurants where I had never eaten, for flowers I had not received, and for jewelry stores from which I owned no jewelry.

When I confronted him with the evidence, he told me I was hysterical over nothing, that I was a stupid woman who had no mind, and that it wasn't true. However, he had gotten involved with someone — a married neighbor woman. She would tell her husband that she was going different places out of town but she was really running around with various men. All the neighbors talked about it. Everyone knew about it except her husband.

I had had enough. The next day, I filed for divorce. There was no thinking about it. I just did it. I was at the attorney's office at 9 o'clock in the morning. It was as though I could survive all the mental and physical abuse but it took another woman to convince me that I was finally through.

Gunter went crazy during the divorce. He threatened to kill me. He was so violent that my attorney had to put a restraining order on him. When my attorney and accountant looked through my affairs, they told me that I was penniless. Gunter owned everything: my condo, my furniture, my art collection, my car, even my business. All the things I had bought and paid for were legally in his name. It took a lot of effort for me to get enough money to live on while I prepared to start over. Fortunately, most of my clients stayed with me and after a period of years I was able to bounce back. But at that moment life looked pretty bleak.

On top of that, there were the bills. Gunter had charged incredible bills to all of my accounts. I had no idea when he had stolen my credit cards and used them, but he had overwhelmed me with debts. More than that, he had borrowed large sums of money in my name.

My attorney tried to be encouraging, but the judge neither knew nor cared about the problems of battered women. Since the bills were on my credit cards or in my name, he awarded all Gunter's debts to me. I had lost my business, my home, and now I lost my credit without which it was almost impossible for me to function. Not only was I penniless, but I owed vast sums to Gunter's creditors! To make matters worse, even after all the evidence that he was a dangerous, abusive, and violent man, the judge allowed Gunter liberal visiting privileges with our little boy.

There was nothing I could do. I always refused to see him in person, but he continued to be verbally abusive on the phone. I was advised never to allow him into my house. When he came to pick up my son, I would open the door, tell him the boy would be out in a minute, and close the door in his face. Although he continued to live and entertain extravagantly, he never paid a penny in child support unless I took him to court and pressed for payment. This was time-consuming and expensive and after a while, I just gave up. The day my son celebrated his eighteenth birthday and was no longer bound by the court orders, he refused to see his father ever again.

I had heard people talk about women's shelters, but I thought they were only accessible for really poor women, and so I did not even think about going there. I went to a psychiatrist for follow-up visits after my divorce. As far as I know, he had no training in dealing with the special problems of battered women. He was an older gentleman who was used to working with childhood and teenage problems. He kept demanding to know what I thought I had done that I needed to be punished for the rest of my life. He kept saying that I was a masochist and had brought all of this trouble on myself.

Now I know that this was the ignorant nonsense of a man who was not familiar with my problems, but at that time I was seeking help and he was not helping me. The one thing he told me that was helpful was when he said, "A divorce is a shock to anybody, It's just like a death. It can upset a person's system. In the case of an abused woman, it takes a little bit longer for recovery, for getting back into a normal world."

I associated my experience with what life must have been like for people who lived in concentration camps or prisoner of war camps. My mind was unbelievably messed up. I knew I would grieve for a long time, but I didn't realize how long. Although my friends and family encouraged me to socialize, I felt that I had enough problems to deal with, and I didn't believe I could deal with men. But being all alone hurt so badly I could hardly stand it. My friends and family didn't give up on me. I finally recovered sufficiently to feel comfortable talking with people. Little by little, I began to socialize. I went to parties and eventually began to date again. When that happened, I realized that I could have good times. Finally, I really was in control of my life again.

Gunter convinced me that I couldn't do a lot of things that I know I can do because I was doing them all along. I can spearhead a successful business. I can make decisions. I can support myself and my son. Now that I am on my own, I am a far stronger and happier person.

What Happened

Although Gunter was awarded all Casey's assets, he quickly squandered them and was forced to return to Europe where he works for a former business associate. He has remarried and is abusing his new wife. Casey's business is thriving. Through hard work and dynamic energy, she has overcome her financial difficulties and replaced all she lost. She is sending her son to an Ivy League school. Although her ulcer is cured and her health has returned, she is still afraid of enclosed spaces, cannot fly, and can scarcely drive on a freeway. Although she is now comfortable in social situations and is frequently seen on the society pages, she is not ready to make another permanent commitment.

7

Julia

THE FAMILY'S POINT OF VIEW

Julia's story is told from the point of view of her frightened family, good people unfamiliar with domestic violence. It demonstrates the fear and confusion that family members feel as they come to suspect and finally to believe that abuse is taking place. Even then, family members may not know when to intervene or how to help the victim of abuse.

Julia was the beautiful sister. She was the smart sister. Unfortunately, she was also the unmarried sister, and at thirty, being an "old maid" canceled out all the honor and glory her academic career had brought to her large, ethnic family. In their collective opinion, the only acceptable occupation for a pretty young woman was wife-and-mother. Her career as a professor at a major university was only a job to her aunts, uncles, and cousins, who were constantly calling lonely bachelors and well-fixed widowers to her attention.

So it was with the greatest pleasure that the family learned about Julia's gentleman friend. Morley had walked into her life and swept Julia off her feet. She blushed with excitement and giggled like a schoolgirl when she spoke his name.

To everyone's surprise, Morley was unattractive, not particularly clean, and remarkably ill-mannered. He spoke of nothing but himself, his talents, his abilities, his wealth, and his family. He told them he had graduate degrees and was fluent in Latin, Greek, Arabic, Hebrew, and Sanskrit. He said his wife and children had been killed in a terrible car wreck that had almost destroyed his life and that he had taken leave of his college professorship to write a book about this sad experience. The book would be published within a month, after which he would return to teaching at the university while he worked at several promising businesses he owned.

No one was particularly taken with Morley, but no one dared admit it. Julia had waited so long to find love that they were willing to accept him, if only he would make her happy.

Morley and Julia announced their engagement, and Morley declared he would buy Julia an engagement ring within the week. But Morley only used the promise of the ring as an opportunity to rage against Julia's family, shouting that they were more interested in symbols than in relationships. When Julia protested, Morley shoved her and shouted at her. Hours of shoving and shouting were followed by his contrite apologies and professions of love.

The ring had not yet appeared on her finger when Julia appeared on her sister Maria's doorstep late at night. She didn't mention Morley's outburst. "Morley wants to be married right away," Julia said. "When I tell him I've always wanted a big wedding, he says, 'Don't you love me?' I don't know what to do."

"Mamma's a widow. She doesn't have much money," Maria said. "How are you going to pay for a big wedding?"

"I'll pay for it," Julia replied. "I've saved some money over the years."

Maria suggested a simple ceremony followed by a reception at her house. "That way you can wear the white dress without the expense."

"That sounds wonderful!" said Julia, and made arrangements to be married the following Saturday night. The aunts and cousins and other women were engaged in a flurry of cooking and baking, but instead of marrying on Saturday, Morley took Julia and Mamma to the country to meet his family. Mamma had heard so much about his distinguished old family of judges and congressmen with all their wealth and history that she was shocked to find his parents living in a trailer house, surrounded by packed dirt and rooting animals. Although their arrival had been expected, they found Morley's father fast asleep on the sofa in his undershirt. The mother and sisters seemed afraid to disturb him.

"I think this family is not what we were led to believe," Mamma confided to Maria later. "I suspect Morley is not the man he says he is. Perhaps you can talk some sense into Julia."

Maria tried to telephone Julia at her little apartment near the university, but Morley was there. Morley was always there so that Maria could find no time to talk with her sister privately. Morley spoke and Julia kept silent. She never answered a question without turning to him for the answer. It was as though Julia's personality were eroding before their eyes, as though Morley had taken over her will. Distressed, Maria contrived to meet her sister at the university. "Perhaps you should think about this," she said.

"Morley says there's no need to think when you're in love."

"Where does he come from? Where is he going? Perhaps you should get to know more about the man you love."

"We know each other better than any two souls on earth."

"Perhaps you should give this romance some time," Maria said.

"But I love him."

That was all there was to say. It ended the conversation.

Morley changed his mind abruptly and encouraged Julia to have the large, expensive, wedding; in fact, he demanded it, inviting his most casual acquaintances to attend. On the day of the wedding, Morley did not permit Julia to visit with her bridesmaids or her relatives, but kept her busy from early morning until it was time for the procession to begin. He rushed Julia all over town, demanding that she sign checks to pay for the various expenses he had incurred. When she protested, he alternately shouted and raged or pouted, demanding to know whether she wanted to call the wedding off at that late hour. He did not permit her to eat or to rest during the day, so she was completely exhausted when he finally decided they should arrive for the ceremony.

The guests were shocked when Julia appeared looking ashen and drained. She wore the bridal crown of a queen but there was no animation in her actions. She looked like a painted image of herself, as though only her body were there, as though her spirit were somewhere else.

"Listen to me," Maria whispered softly into her ear. "I want you to know that no matter what happens, no matter what Morley tells you, you are my sister and I love you. You can always count on me."

Julia hugged her sister but she did not speak.

Morley's father took his penknife from his pocket and attempted to chip the gold mosaic tiles off the wall. When the wedding procession began, Morley was noticeably drunk. The arrangements were beautiful, the flowers exquisite, and the food abundant at the reception, but Morley shouted and raved at everyone who crossed his path.

In keeping with Old World custom, relatives and guests pinned their wedding gifts of money and checks to Julia's wedding purse. They were shocked to see Morley pull the money from his bride and stuff it greedily into his own pockets. They watched as he forced Julia to drink wine until she was reeling. Finally, Morley grabbed Julia's arm and dragged Julia away from her wedding reception. She slipped and fell. He yanked her up, dragged her roughly across the dance floor in her wedding dress, and pulled her out of the building. Morley threw Julia into his old car and screeched away in a grinding of gears.

"Morley's a dangerous man," Julia's friend Cecile whispered into Maria's ear. "Morley grew up in my old neighborhood. I tried to tell Julia about him but she wouldn't listen. Morley's wife and children aren't dead. His wife ran away because he beat her. And he beat the children, too. He lived with a girl named Belleza. He beat her and she's scarred for life. I tried to tell Julia," Cecile repeated. "I tried . . ."

"She wouldn't listen to me either, Cecile." Maria's voice was calm but there was panic in her heart. Morley and Julia were traveling to Mexico for their honeymoon. What danger was Julia in, in a strange country with a man like that? Maria spent the night calling the airlines, but the airlines found no record of their flight.

Maria had no way of knowing that Julia had never been to Mexico, that Morley had instead taken her to a cheap motel in town. Deprived of food and rest, her clothing hidden from her, Julia was locked in the hotel room, where Morley systematically eroded her self-esteem by repeated batterings interspersed with kind, caring attention and demonstrations of passionate love. By morning, both her eyes were swollen shut, and black-and-blue marks covered most of her body. Morley insisted that she drink large quantities of alcohol to ease her pain.

Meanwhile, Maria had telephoned a family friend who could help them get information.

"This Morley has a police record, and he can be dangerous," the friend soon reported. "You should get your sister away from him as quickly as you can."

They did not hear from Julia for the better part of two weeks. When Julia finally appeared on Mamma's doorstep, she was more subdued than ever. What had she seen on her trip? Where had she eaten? Was the hotel pretty? Were the people friendly? She would say nothing about the honeymoon trip. She was silent.

"You're in danger," Maria whispered to her sister. "You have to get away."

"Oh, you've been talking to Cecile," Julia responded in a monotone. "Morley told me she's jealous of him."

Morley panicked when Julia repeated Maria's words to him at home. Enraged by his inability to control the situation, he beat Julia more than ever before, first knocking her down and then kicking her in the stomach and ribs as she lay bleeding on the floor.

Julia telephoned Maria very late that night. Her voice was strange. "What you said about Morley," she asked, "Do you have documentation on that?"

Maria heard a muffled sound, like a hand covering the telephone. Then there was the sound of another person breathing on the line.

"What you said upset Morley," Julia continued. "He wants you to know that he has never been in any kind of trouble."

Morley seized the phone before Maria could respond. He began to shout obscenities, calling her terrible names. Clearly, he was drunk and out of control. "I am going to get you," he shouted. "I'm going to kill you!"

Shocked, Maria hung up. Julia called back. It was impossible to hear her timid voice above Morley's obscenities and threats.

Maria hung up again.

Julia called back again and again. Morley screamed incoherently, shouting that Cecile and his former wife and his live-in girlfriend were all drug addicts and whores. "If you try to get my police record, I'll know about it and I'll kill you!" he screamed. "I tape every conversation Julia has. I listen to every word she says."

Maria's husband, Tony, took the telephone. "Hang up," he told Morley. "Hang up now, and don't call back."

Julia telephoned Maria the following morning and recited a prepared speech. "Morley wants to tell you that he over-reacted, and he wants to apologize. He wants to call you but he doesn't think you'd speak with him. I love you. I'm not in any danger now. I love him."

"Are we taping this conversation, Julia?"

"Yes, we are."

Julia didn't tell Maria about the hours of violent battering she had endured the previous night. Morley had torn her hair and ripped off her clothing. He had threatened to kill Julia and her relatives.

Maria and Cecile decided to go see Belleza, the girl Morley had lived with and beaten. Her looks were strikingly similar to Julia's, delicate and blonde. But an ugly knife scar ran from her eyebrow to her chin. She was saving money to repair her broken front teeth.

"This is only the most obvious part of it," the girl confided. "Most of the scars have faded now. At least the scars that you can see. I still have the nightmares." She told a tale of emotional and physical degradation. "If I were you, I'd go to the courthouse and find out about his divorce from his first wife."

"Why's that?"

"Because they never got divorced. Morley's still married to her!"

Meanwhile, Julia's personality continued to erode. She only visited when the family insisted she attend a celebration or holiday party. She hardly spoke, always allowing Morley to speak for her. She was like a robot, doing only what Morley told her to do. He never permitted her to be alone with any relative or friend.

Morley memorized Julia's every word and action when they were in the presence of others, and he would force her to stand at attention in the bedroom for hours, explaining herself as he raved about her "subterfuge" and "infidelity." When she was terrified, confused, and totally exhausted, the battering would begin. One night, after they had visited her family, Morley became so enraged that he chased her through their apartment with her heated curling iron, burning her flesh each time he caught her. Later, he became contrite and loving, promising never to hit her again. This time, he insisted she consume large doses of pills to ease her pain.

"Look here," her cousin Vinnie said. "We have a girl who is turned into a zombie. We have a man whose wife and children were killed in a car wreck, but they turn out to be alive. We have a man who has a book being published, but there is no book. We have a man who has businesses, but he never goes to work and he has no income from these businesses. I have a feeling that we don't know the worst of it."

"And I say we do something about it." Maria looked at him levelly. "I met a man who said he worked with Morley once. I'll talk to him."

When she met with him later that week, he laughed.

"It wasn't at any college. You think I teach in a college? I work in a factory! I worked with Morley in a factory two years ago." The man told how Morley had boasted of supplying large amounts of "Lebanese hash, pot, coke, and other drugs."

Maria was shocked, but not nearly so shocked as when the man produced a copy of the factory newsletter announcing that Morley had married still another woman one year to the day before he had married Julia!

Maria went to Julia's neat little apartment near the university to confront Morley with this information. But the apartment was empty. No books, no furniture, no clothes. Julia was gone.

"I don't know where she went, but she's gone," Maria told her mother.

"I'll bet I know where she is." Mamma telephoned Morley's parents at the trailer house in the country.

After initially denying Julia's presence, Morley's mother finally called Julia to the phone. Her voice was so weak she could barely be heard, and before she could say much Morley grabbed the phone. He did the talking for the two of them. "Julia quit her job at the university and we decided to leave the city. We're married people, and we can go anywhere we want to go. There's nothing you can do about it."

But Julia had not quit her job at the university. She had been dismissed. Morley had somehow convinced her to allow him to teach her classes. Realizing that the man was incoherent, her graduate students complained to the department head. Julia was warned, but she continued to allow Morley to teach her classes. This action, combined with her increasingly bizarre behavior, left the university no alternative but to dismiss her.

Maria learned that Morley had no college degrees of any kind. The universities he had named had never heard of him. But he did have a police record with convictions for drug possession. His driver's license had been suspended for a DWI conviction.

At the courthouse, Cecile found a record of Morley's marriage to the second wife. There was no record of a divorce from the second wife, but the divorce from his first wife became final the day before he married Julia.

The first wife had obtained a divorce by publication. She had hunted for him. She had even appeared on their doorstep and pleaded with his parents to tell her where to locate him, but she could never find him to make him appear in court. Child support would be assessed if and when he was ever found.

Meanwhile, Vinnie learned that Morley was still involved with drugs, "off and on. Dealing in a small-time way. He acts as a 'mule,' a transporter. He could be feeding Julia drugs, with or without her knowing it."

One day, Maria noticed Morley's shabby old car parked near Mamma's house. Inside were many of Julia's wedding gifts, still in their wrapping, Morley's greasy old jacket, and Julia's treasured leather briefcase, stuffed with her papers, syllabus, and books.

The car was still registered to the woman who had sold it to Morley. He had never changed the legal registration or license plates. Because of his police record, he habitually drove with another person's title until the plates expired. Then he abandoned the car with everything in it on the street.

Then, after months of silence, Maria was astonished to hear her sister's voice on the phone. "You'll have to stop upsetting Mamma," Julia said angrily. "I don't know what's going on with you. You tell her all these rumors about Morley that aren't true."

"There are no rumors, only the truth."

"All I know is that Morley has to protect me from you because you're so mean to me."

"I'm mean to you?"

"You are. Morley only gets upset because he thinks someone is hurting me."

"Use your head, Julia," Maria said. "Try to think like a normal person. Morley threatened to kill me! That's not normal. Something weird is going on."

"Oh no," Julia said, "nothing weird is going on. Now that I've finally got someone who will stand by me and love me and take care of things for me, my family is trying to ruin my life."

After this phone conversation, Maria tried to reason with her sister in a letter. She didn't know that Morley intercepted the mail and hid Julia's checks, bills, letters, and cards.

Then the telephone company sent Mamma a form to sign that would guarantee payment for Morley and Julia's telephone bill. She refused to sign it. The jeweler called Mamma for payment on Julia's wedding ring. Morley had never paid for it, and they would be forced to repossess. Mamma told them to go ahead and repossess. A department store called Mamma to ask where Julia lived. Mamma realized they were trying to check up on a bad debt. Julia now owed several hundred dollars in unpaid bills, although she had never owed a cent before she married Morley. The family couldn't know that Morley had stolen Julia's credit cards and was using them to run up huge bills in her name. Having spent every last penny of the money they received as wedding gifts, Morley was without funds. He began forcing Julia to write bad checks. If she refused, she was brutally beaten. He would follow her into a grocery store with a knife or pistol concealed in his pocket and force her to write bad checks at gunpoint. The police were beginning to search for Julia, attempting to serve her with warrants for the bad checks. Morley told the terrified Julia that now she would have to do anything and everything he said without question because she was a fugitive from the law and he was her only protection.

Then Mamma received a notice from the bank. Morley had written two hot checks to Julia for more than $1,000. Julia had cashed them on an old joint account which she and Mamma shared. The bank took the money out of Mamma's account. Mamma closed the joint account. When he heard she had closed the account, Morley began swearing and shouting at Mamma. He said he would no longer permit Julia to visit her.

"Why are you doing this to me?" Julia asked. "Why won't my family accept Morley? His family loves me. Why don't you love him?"

THE BATTERED WOMAN'S SURVIVAL GUIDE

Julia told Mamma she had to accept Morley or she would no longer consider her to be her mother. She said Morley's mother was more of a mother to her than her own, and his sisters were her sisters now. She didn't need Maria anymore. They couldn't know that to get her to tell her mother this, Morley had twisted Julia's arm until the tendons tore, but this was too much for them to take.

"We have to find a way to get her away from him," Maria said. This thing has gone far enough."

"She's over twenty-one. You can't take her away if she doesn't want to go," Tony warned. "They say that people have to reach bottom before they can start back up again."

"I don't know how much lower she can go," Maria sighed.

In fact, Maria could not have imagined the depths of horror to which Julia had already been introduced. When he beat her so black and blue that he didn't want her to be seen in public, Morley locked Julia in the unheated shed attached to his parents' trailer house.

The men in Julia's family actually talked about kidnapping her when an unmarked envelope arrived at Maria's house. Maria knew before she opened it that it was from Morley. There was no note inside—only a photograph of Morley holding a pistol to Julia's head.

Morley frequently held the loaded pistol to Julia's head, threatening to kill her if she so much as thought about leaving him.

They didn't hear anything from Julia after that. The days turned into weeks. Mamma was terrified. "We know how crazy he is. Who knows what he could do? For all we know he could have killed her."

"The police record says he hasn't killed anybody yet," Maria attempted to reassure her. "She's probably all right."

Morley and Julia arrived at Mamma's house. Morley said the windstorm had shut off their electricity and they had to have a place to stay. Julia was sick and coughing badly. Mamma was afraid to let them in, but she was also afraid to turn them away. She gave them money and told them to stay in a motel. She did not know that they were hiding from the police.

Once again, the family did not hear a word for weeks. When Julia finally called, she sounded strong and coherent, like her old self. Morley was not with her. He had somehow found a job which required him to take an apartment in a little country town. Julia had walked to the public library where there was a telephone.

"I love you and I want to see you," Mamma said. "Why don't Maria and I come there and meet you for lunch?"

"I can't do that."

"In other words, Morley won't allow it?" Mamma said.

They did not realize how terrified Julia was of angering Morley. In his last rage, Morley had attempted to beat Julia to death. He had blackened both her eyes. He used his lit cigarette to burn her. He split her lip and broke her front teeth. He attempted to strangle her, grasping her throat, shaking and squeezing, and stopped only when she finally lost consciousness. She had awakened in the morning with the fingerprints of his attempted strangulation still clearly outlined on her throat.

Julia called Mamma again the next day. Once again, she sounded like her old self. Mamma told her she loved her and wanted to see her. When Julia replied that she loved Mamma, she began to cry. Could this be a step in the right direction?

Mamma didn't know that Julia had found a book about battered women in the public library and had begun to understand what was happening to her.

The next time Julia called Mamma she admitted Morley had no idea she was calling. Mamma told her she was not alone in the world. She had a family who loved her.

"Maria hates me," Julia protested.

"I don't care what Morley told you. Your sister loves you," Mamma said.

Suddenly the situation became grimmer. Morley and his father found Julia's borrowed library books and locked them in the trunk of the car to prevent her from returning to the public library. But the library had reminded Julia of the normal life she had once lived, and for the first time she tried to fight back. This so enraged Morley that he beat her brutally. She fought harder and, in the struggle, he bit off the end of her finger.

The next day, Maria's telephone rang.

"Maria," Julia's soft voice was tiny, hardly recognizable in the telephone receiver. "I don't know if you even want to talk to me . . ."

"Julia!" Maria shouted. "Thank God you're alive! Where are you?"

"I'm in a telephone booth . . ." Julia whispered, "I don't know what to do."

"I'll tell you what to do," Maria said as calmly as she could. "Come home."

"It's not as easy as that . . ."

"Do you have any money? Are you near a bus station?"

"Morley left his car in front of the house today," Julia whispered. "He doesn't know it, but I have the keys."

"Then I'll tell you what to do. You put your little backside in that little car and you come to my house right now, this minute."

"I can't do that," Julia said.

"Why not?"

"I don't know."

"So do it."

"OK."

"Come home."

"OK."

"You're going to be all right."

An hour later, Maria saw an unfamiliar figure on her porch. The golden hair was burned by a bad home perm. The front teeth were broken and uneven, and the cheap makeup was heavily applied to hide the black eyes, bruises, and fingerprints. But it was Julia. Her eyes were full of fear, but they were clear, and she spoke with her own voice.

The family finally learned about the horrors, the terror, and the degradation Julia had suffered. Julia would have to start over, but she was alive. The family closed ranks around her. Julia had escaped.

What Happened

Considering Julia's fragile physical and emotional state, her attorney advised against charging Morley with bigamy or attempted murder. Instead, immediate divorce proceedings were begun. Although he was located and served with papers, Morley did not appear in court and was charged with contempt. The judge assessed a sizable divorce settlement with interest compounded daily at the highest possible rate. After the divorce was final the judge took Julia's hand gently and told her he didn't expect her to see a penny of the money, but that the threat of the settlement would keep Morley away from her.

The judge who heard the criminal charges for writing hot checks and credit card fraud was not familiar with problems of family violence and would not consider the fact that Julia did these things under threat of death. He charged her with the responsibility of paying all the debts.

Julia entered counseling at the local battered women's shelter, and is now paying off Morley's enormous bills. The university reinstated her and, in addition to teaching, she is working at two and often three additional jobs. Morley has never paid a penny of the divorce settlement. He has suffered neither financial retribution nor punishment for his crimes. He has remarried and is battering his new wife.

Part Three

HOW TO FIND HELP

8

The Man's Not Worth Shooting

THE LEGAL SYSTEM AND LEGAL RIGHTS

When Battered Women Fight Back

Suppose a woman has just survived a battering episode. The man in her life has beaten her until she is black and blue. The beatings have been getting worse, and they've been happening more often lately. She's afraid to do anything because he's convinced her that he knows everything she says or thinks even before she says or thinks it. He's threatened to kill her, her parents, and her children if she so much as thinks about leaving him. She has no money and no place to go. Her head hurts so badly that she can't think straight, but she starts to imagine what life would be like without him. Her reason and judgment are consumed with only one thing: finding a way to make him stop. She's scared and desperate and doesn't know where to turn. Sometimes she thinks she'd be better off if he were dead.

Forget it.

The man's not worth shooting.

If she attempts to kill him, she might miss and simply wound him, and then he could turn around and kill or handicap her. Then where would she be? Worse, where would her family and her children be? They would all be completely at his mercy, that's where.

Worse, she might actually kill him. Then where would she be? She'd be in prison. And what would become of her family and her children?

Besides, she is not really a violent person, even though the batterer may have convinced her that she is. And she would have to live with the consequences of her actions for the rest of her life. Worse, her family and her children would have to live with those consequences.

To be honest, there is a good chance that society will allow him to get away scot-free, that it will not punish him for what what he has done to her. That's not fair, but that's the way it is. The fact that many batterers suffer no legal punishment for their violence is a disgrace, but it is not the most important thing for the battered woman to consider. What is most important is that she find a way to begin building a new life.

She has to find a legal way out of her troubles.

The Legal System Isn't Perfect

Unfortunately, the experiences of many battered women cause them to believe that the legal system takes up where the batterer leaves off. The legal system is only beginning to come to terms with the Battered Woman Syndrome. It still must work through long-established guidelines about what is right and wrong in domestic situations. It is only now beginning to confront the hardships that many battered women face in their search for justice.

Men who kill their wives frequently commit murder during a fit of anger or jealousy, which is viewed by the law as a crime of passion. Many of the battered women who kill their husbands think about it for a long time and plan it before they do it. Whether it is called first-degree manslaughter or homicide or something else altogether, it is considered to be premeditated murder, and that carries a much heavier sentence than does a "crime of passion." Prisons are full of women who were victims of violence and who responded with violence.

The battered woman doesn't need to join them.

There is also a serious form of gender bias in the laws of self-defense, which were originally designed to deal with barroom brawls between two men of equal strength, not with life-and-death battles between a 225-pound man and a 110-pound woman.

Although it would be unfair to have separate laws for men and women, a disparity in physical size should be a consideration in situations of self-defense. Yet judges and attorneys often see only the legal solutions and not the real life results of those solutions.

Many judges and attorneys believe the unfairness battered women so often face is not inherent in the law but only in the way it is applied. They believe inequities result from the variety of people who are involved in the system, including the judges, lawyers, and litigants. They are convinced that the existing laws are sufficient to deal with domestic violence. Battered women do not share this belief in the system. They know from experience what its results are.

Amy

When Amy's husband tried to cut her throat with his hunting knife, she fought for her life and accidentally killed him in the struggle. She was convicted of murder and sentenced to prison.

Elaine

Elaine's former husband was a heavy drug user, and he also sold illegal drugs. A criminal court convicted him of drug trafficking, but he got off with a large fine and a probated sentence. Paying the fine posed no difficulty for a man who was rapidly growing wealthy through his drug dealings. He considered the fine a business expense.

Elaine, on the other hand, found herself supporting her children after the divorce by working at two minimum-wage jobs. She worked as a waitress during the day and as a scrub-woman for a cleaning service at night. Since it was easy for her former husband to demonstrate his financial stability with large bank accounts, extensive investments, a fine house, and several expensive cars, the domestic court awarded this convicted drug dealer sole custody of their three impressionable youngsters.

Nell

The brutality of the abuse she endured left Nell moderately disabled and permanently unable to work to support herself. The court awarded her a large financial settlement with the intention of providing for her needs. She has never seen one cent of the money.

THE BATTERED WOMAN'S SURVIVAL GUIDE

Debbie

After ransacking her apartment and vandalizing her car, Debbie's former husband left messages on her telephone answering machine threatening her life and the life of their baby, including such threats as, "You are going to disappear like Jimmy Hoffa." The judge, who listened to the recordings, granted her former husband unsupervised visitation privileges. Debbie is terrified each time her former husband takes her baby from her arms. She never knows whether she will see her child alive again.

Laurel

Laurel's former husband stole her life savings, destroyed her credit, and left her destitute. The court ordered her to pay all the debts he had accrued during their brief marriage. While she is now subsisting at the poverty level while working at two jobs to pay these debts, her former husband has started a new business and paid cash for a new car.

Carol

Carol's former husband never makes court-ordered child support payments. Because of his violent behavior, he is allowed to see the children only in her home with her supervision. He comes into her apartment every Sunday afternoon, watches her TV, becomes unruly and breaks her furniture, and eats all the food she bought on her small salary, leaving the family to go hungry the rest of the week.

Carol is afraid to complain to the court for fear a new hearing will somehow award this dangerous man unsupervised visitation rights.

Sally

Sally's former husband has repeatedly broken into her apartment, stolen her money, destroyed her property, threatened her, and beaten her brutally. He has repeatedly violated the orders which have been issued to protect her from his violence. Last time she called the police they took more than two hours to respond to her desperate pleas for help. By the time they arrived, Sally's apartment was completely destroyed and Sally was in the hospital.

Nancy

Nancy's live-in lover repeatedly abused her and threatened to kill her and her young teenage son if she ever reported the abuse. She was suffering from the typical battered woman's paralysis of will by the time her lover turned his rage against her son. During a particularly violent episode, she summoned all her courage and told the boy to run and hide, but he stayed and tried to protect his mother.

The boy was quickly overpowered. During the following hours, the boy was bound and gagged with tape and beaten with a baseball bat, a hammer, a wine bottle, and fists. He was scalded with hot water, burned with matches, and had his head slammed against a wall and his hair pulled out. While the terrorized mother watched her son die, her lover insisted the boy was "only pretending to be dead" and burned matches under his nose, attempting to force him to respond.

Since she did not report the fact that her son was being physically abused until after he was dead, Nancy was charged with murder, for which she could have been imprisoned for life. Instead, the jury found her guilty of involuntary manslaughter for which she must serve ten years in jail.

These stories are horrible . . . and true.

The Legal Way Out

The laws regarding domestic violence desperately need to be changed to accommodate the special problems of battered women and the violent men who batter them.

In the past, our legal system has dealt badly with problems of family violence. This may be the result of old ideas about privacy and about not interfering in the special relationship between a man and his wife. It may be that there is simply a lack of understanding about battered women on the part of some peace officers, lawyers, and judges.

Although these individuals may deal with battered women, many of them don't really understand what family violence is all about. They still ask such questions as, "Why didn't she just leave? Why didn't she ask for help?" Legal reforms are needed that will make the system fairer, less punitive, and perhaps even gentler for battered women involved in crimes.

These reforms must deal not only with those who kill their batterers but also with women who are forced by their batterers to write hot checks, commit theft, traffic in illegal drugs, engage in prostitution, and commit other such crimes under severe duress.

But some laws are already in place to protect battered women in some communities. And laws—and attitudes—elsewhere are changing.

No matter what the man in her life has told her, or done to her, or forced her to do, the battered woman *must* seek a legal way out of her troubles. She and her attorney will have to step carefully through this potential mine field and weigh precisely what is and is not in her interest. But, although she may not know it, she does have recourse under the law.

Police Involvement

If the battered woman is not a lawyer, she may not know that family laws are different in different states. Unless they are specifically outlined by the state, such laws may also be different in different towns, cities, and neighborhoods. The way a battered woman is treated may even depend upon the attitude of the police officer sent to help her. Some officers are well trained to deal with domestic violence, while others have no training at all.

The police situation is changing. The 9th Circuit Court of Appeals has recently held that a spouse may sue the police for failing to respond to domestic violence calls when a "special relationship" has been established between the spouse and the law enforcement agencies. An example of this special relationship may be a protective order. The Court's analysis rests chiefly on a spouse's right to due process of law. The 10th Circuit Court has held that a spouse may prevail under the right to equal protection of the law, by showing through statistical evidence that the local police were indifferent to the domestic violence.

Because family violence is so widespread, many states have sought to fight this silent epidemic by passing major domestic violence laws. Many cities have mandatory police training classes in techniques for dealing with domestic violence. Some cities have established crisis intervention teams made up of police officers and civilian counselors. Everywhere that police officers have received this training or worked with the staffs of women's shelters, they have become more sensitive to the problems of battered women.

In most places, any time one person threatens or hurts another person, the police are required to prevent further injuries and stop attempts to cause injuries. In many places, if the law enforcement officials see evidence of an injury such as a black eye, a bloodied nose, broken bones, wounds from guns, knives, or other weapons, or any injury serious enough to need emergency medical care, they can arrest the batterer immediately without a warrant. If they see that a misdemeanor assault has been committed and that the victim is in danger of continued assault, again they can arrest the batterer immediately without a warrant.

Such an assault may be considered a felony. But if the police have been called out for domestic violence that is less dramatic and offers less evidence of severe physical assault, they may choose not to make an arrest. Even though it may be difficult, a battered woman should always write down the officers' names and badge numbers in case she needs them as witnesses or for information later. If she is hospitalized or receives emergency medical treatment, she should keep medical records, bills, and other documents as evidence. The physically abused woman should arrange to photograph her injuries immediately after the attack. As difficult as that may be at the time, it will be very helpful to her at the hearing.

It is a myth that domestic violence calls are the most dangerous calls police officers can make. Officers are in considerably more danger facing a perpetrator armed with an automatic weapon than they are defending an unarmed woman against a batterer.

However, most officers will agree that domestic violence calls are among the most unpleasant calls they make. The situation is murky, volatile, and unpredictable. Even in cities that provide training programs in dealing with domestic violence, many officers may still consider such violence to be a family problem rather than criminal activity. Many officers have had the unfortunate experience of trying to assist a battered woman only to have her turn violently against them to protect her batterer! Or they may have rescued her only to have her insist she does not need their help. Many officers do not understand her fear, or fear of the reprisals she will suffer when they leave. Often, battered women do not realize they *do* have certain legal rights which can offer limited protection for them and their children.

Criminal Charges

As a victim of domestic violence, a woman may decide she wants to file criminal charges against her batterer. If so, she will have to go to the police station and sign a complaint.

The "official" response to her decision to file depends on where she lives. She may be told it will be a waste of time for her to swear out a complaint because most women only drop their complaints when they cool down. She may be told to think about it for ten days and come back if she still wants to file a complaint. Or she may be advised not to initiate an arrest because when her batterer is released on bail, he will be even angrier and will beat her again.

These excuses are often given by police officers and even by county and district attorneys for not acting to protect victims of domestic violence. But is any other victim of violent crime obliged to wait ten days before signing a complaint or discouraged from seeking protection under the law? Of course not. These excuses are used as delaying tactics only in situations of family violence.

It is true that many battered women have dropped charges in the past, and many more will do so in the future. They may fear the renewed threats of their batterers or enter the honeymoon phase of the cycle and become more confused and dependent. Instead of dissuading battered women from filing and pursuing charges, law enforcement should help to ensure that such charges *are* filed and such cases *are* prosecuted.

Some prosecutor's offices have adopted "no-drop" policies for victims of domestic violence, so that once a battered woman files charges against her batterer, her request for dismissal is automatically denied. This shifts the responsibility for prosecuting the batterer from the weakened shoulders of the victim to those of the state. Some prosecutor's offices also offer support and assistance to the battered woman. They refer her to local agencies for counseling and shelter, so the battered woman can be protected and set on the road to a normal life.

Assault and Battery

Assault is a misdemeanor. The law punishes a misdemeanor by fine or imprisonment or both. People commit assault if they threaten another person with bodily injury and put that person in fear of imminent bodily harm, or if they cause physical contact with another person when they know or understand that the person they contact will regard the contact as offensive or provocative. This includes threatening or making any unwelcome contact with family members. People commit battery if they injure another person's body through physical injury or offensive touching, or any physical contact causing pain, illness, or any impairment of physical condition. This includes injuring a family member.

Assault With a Dangerous or Deadly Weapon

Lawyers describe assault with a dangerous or deadly weapon as an unlawful attempt or offer to do bodily harm without justification or excuse by use of any instrument calculated to do harm or cause death. Assault with a deadly weapon such a gun or knife which causes serious bodily injury is a felony. The law punishes a felony by confinement in a penitentiary or by the death penalty.

Civil Law

Civil law governs the rights, responsibilities, and duties of parties involved in legal relationships. Rights in civil law depend for their enforcement on the individuals involved. In civil law, the parties involved have the right to sue or not to sue. However, criminal law governs the behavior of individuals and relies on the government for its enforcement. In criminal cases, it is the state or municipality that has the right to sue or not to sue. Laws can place different degrees of restrictions on what a batterer can or cannot do when it comes to contacting his partner and his family. Each instrument of law has features that may be strengths or weaknesses in a particular situation.

It is important to remember that different states, cities, and towns have different laws. Not all of the following information applies to all locations. The advice of an attorney who understands both the local laws and special problems of domestic violence is absolutely essential for a battered woman.

If she has enough money to hire private legal counsel, she should look for a lawyer she likes and understands as well as one who understands her and the special problems of domestic violence.

Even if she has little or no money, she can find a lawyer

willing to work with her.

The kindly old family lawyer may not be the best choice to help a battered woman because he or she may not be experienced in handling the special problems of family violence. Social workers, shelter workers, counselors, and Legal Aid Societies may be able to recommend lawyers who are experts in this type of family law.

Peace Bond

A Peace Bond can be issued by a Justice of the Peace to protect a woman being threatened with a crime. She will have to appear before the justice and make a formal statement of why she believes that, if not stopped, the batterer will injure her.

In some cases the Justice of the Peace can then set a hearing date and give the batterer legal right and opportunity to explain. Or the Justice of the Peace may issue a warrant for the batterer's arrest and hear evidence about the accusations after the arrest is made.

If the Justice of the Peace is satisfied that the batterer intended to carry out the threat when he made it, a Peace Bond will be issued. The batterer puts up money, which will be forfeited to the state if the threat is carried out.

Peace Bonds are valid for up to one year and contain specific conditions, such as banning the batterer from making threatening phone calls or from contacting the woman at home or work. If the batterer refuses to post bond, he may be jailed for up to one year or until bond is posted. A Peace Bond is only a solution for threats, not for violence. If a crime threat has been carried out, a criminal complaint rather than a Peace Bond should be filed.

Peace Bonds are most useful when the woman does not live with or is not married to the batterer. The court should be asked for Protective Orders when she is married to or living with the batterer.

Protective Order

A Protective Order is a legal paper designed to protect victims of domestic violence. It is available to family or household members related by blood or marriage, biological parents of the same child, former spouses, foster children, and foster parents.

A Protective Order can bar a person or his agents from

committing family violence, directly threatening or harassing a family or household member, or going to or near the protected person's home or workplace, as specifically outlined in the Protective Order. Knowing or intentional violation of the order is a misdemeanor.

This legal remedy is separate from a divorce action and should be used when divorce is not desirable or appropriate, when family members need court protection, or when the people involved are not married.

Temporary Protective Order
A Temporary Protective Order may be issued by a court and combined with divorce proceedings when a divorce is pending. It can be in effect at least twenty days before the divorce hearing and last up to one year after the hearing. A district attorney or county attorney can help a woman get a Temporary Protective Order, the police receive notification of it, and a violation of it is punishable as a criminal offense and as contempt of court.

Temporary Restraining Order
A Temporary Restraining Order is issued by a court without notice to the other party and restrains affected parties from engaging in specific kinds of conduct. This must be part of a divorce and must be requested by the victim or her lawyer. The police do not receive notification of it, and violation of it involves no criminal penalties. Rather, violation of this order is punishable by contempt of court. In many states, the defendant must appear within a certain number of days from the date the order is issued and "show cause" why the order ought not be continued while the case is pending. Restraining orders are called Temporary Injunctions after the hearing and Permanent Injunctions after the divorce.

Her Responsibilities
If a court grants a battered woman a Protective Order or a Restraining Order, she is also bound by its provisions. If the order does not allow the batterer to enter her house, she should never allow him to come in under any circumstances. If he is allowed to visit her children, she should ask the court to order him to visit them in a specified place outside her house. She can lose her rights to protection if she does not comply. If the batterer does not

comply, she must report the violation to her lawyer and the court immediately.

A warning: It is important to understand that the papers themselves cannot protect her. The batterer may be jailed once he has violated the orders, but by that time the battered woman may be hurt—or worse.

Divorce

Divorce, the legal dissolving of a marriage, includes the division of possessions and property as well as debts, grants custody of children, and orders any child support.

In most places the batterer must be given a copy of the divorce petition and of any Temporary Restraining Order. If he refuses to sign a statement that he has been given copies of these papers, the sheriff or constable can deliver the papers to him and sign the statement saying that he has been given a copy.

If a woman is awarded a property judgment as part of her divorce, she should ask to have the judgment abstracted in every county where her former husband owns or may own property.

She should ask her lawyer about other specific protections and rights which the law provides for her as a post-judgment creditor, such as a Writ of Garnishment by which her former partner's bank account may be garnished or a Writ of Turnover by which his paycheck may be turned over to her. A judgment in a divorce case is as binding as in any civil case, but no judgment is self-executing. Its enforcement depends solely on the efforts of the person who gets the judgment. Although many battered women fear any further contact and live in fear of possible retribution by their former husbands, the owner of a judgment must be relentless. Bills of discovery, asset hearings, contempt proceedings, or garnishment may be essential.

Child Support

Although law enforcement agencies in some states are not always strict about enforcing payments, child support is a binding debt. It is not even dischargeable by bankruptcy.

If a battered woman can afford to support her children without receiving child support, she can terminate his rights to the child. Termination of his parental rights ends his visitation rights and his child support responsibilities. Parental rights laws vary by state.

Termination of his rights should be considered anytime the batterer has a history of child abuse. Some courts may favor it as a way of resolving dangerous situations. Other courts are biased toward keeping the family intact and may refuse termination even under astonishing circumstances.

Civil Lawsuit

If a battered woman chooses to file a civil lawsuit for damages caused by abuse or assault, it is possible that a court may award her money for medical expenses, mental and physical suffering and attorney's fees. It is also possible that the court will award her nothing. She and her attorney should discuss the special problems of battered women, domestic violence, and civil lawsuits before she decides to sue. Many attorneys advise against doing so because of additional emotional strain for the woman and her children.

Her Best Interests

Most attorneys and advocates for battered women understand that their clients are in a precarious emotional state. Although there may be enough evidence for criminal or civil lawsuits or bigamy charges against a batterer, many attorneys will advise against bringing such suits.

In giving this advice, they may agree with a noted district court judge who said, "Any woman involved with a 'beater' needs to get free of him as quickly and painlessly as possible so that she can go on with the work of rebuilding her life."

The attitude that neither retribution nor restitution is as important as reclaiming a normal life may be valid for the woman and her family. That is something only she can decide, and she can only decide once she is free from the battering situation. Until then, she should know that the law gives her the right to be protected from assault.

The battered woman must remember that even though she has lived in a violent situation, she did not create it. She is not a violent person. No matter how long she has been told that she is stupid, ignorant, and worthless, no matter how perverse the things the batterer has done to her or has forced her to do, she is still a decent person with a life worth reclaiming.

Once she has separated herself from the battering situation, the man in her life may decide to go into counseling so that he can learn to control his antisocial behavior. He may decide that he is not interested in counseling and is happy living his life in the way he has been living it.

His choice is not her problem.

Her problem is reconstructing her life and reclaiming her self-worth.

That is her choice to make.

Choose life.

9

What Happens When She Seeks Help

Finding Help

Suppose the last battering incident was so horrible that the woman is finally convinced that she must do something to preserve the last shattered remnants of her life. Suppose she has somehow managed to overcome her doubts and fears. Suppose she has finally worked up the courage to ask for help. What can she expect? What will happen once the process of rebuilding her own life begins? Where does she start? What will become of her?

Her Church

The first thing she must do is to find help. She may wish to go to the church or synagogue of her faith. It doesn't matter if the man in her life has not allowed her to worship there for many years. She can go there anyway.

She can explain her problem to her clergyman and ask for the address of the battered women's shelter or family crisis center nearest her home. It is sad, but she must be very careful about listening to the advice she gets. The clergy is made up of human beings and, like all human beings, some will be more kind and caring than others. Some will be well-informed about the problems of domestic violence and the needs of battered women, and some simply will not understand.

If she finds herself talking to a cleric who tells her that she is the cause of all her problems, or that she should go home and pray for guidance to become a better woman, or that she should go home and pray for forgiveness because she questioned her husband's authority, or that she should go home and pray for the Lord to make her husband a better person, or that she is making it all up and she doesn't mean what she is saying, she should thank him or her politely and get up and leave.

She must not pay any attention to what she has been told. These are not the correct answers for her problem. She needs to find a humane religious advisor who is aware of the problems of domestic violence and who can help her, not one who makes her feel guilty.

A Counselor

She must remember the same thing when she visits a psychologist, psychiatrist, family therapist, or any other kind of counselor. These professionals may know a great deal about their particular fields, but some will be familiar with the problems battered women face and some will not. A battered woman will be able to tell the difference.

If her counselor tells her that she is the cause of all her problems, or that something happened in her early childhood to bring these problems down on her, or that people attract the problems they want to have, she should thank him or her politely and get up and leave.

The Hospital

If she winds up in the hospital as a result of battering, a woman should tell the doctor and hospital personnel what really happened to her. And she shouldn't be surprised if the nature of her wounds has already told the medical personnel the whole story. They have seen it all before. She can tell them she is in real danger and ask them to contact a representative of the local family crisis center or women's shelter. Trained volunteers from the women's center will be able to visit her in the hospital. They won't be shocked or amazed by what has happened to her because they too have seen it all before. They can explain her options, offer support, and provide referral information.

The Police

If a woman is in acute danger, and the man in her life has not yet managed to find a way to get her into trouble with the law, she can call the police.

Every state has different laws dealing with families. Every city and town has its own laws. In some places the police are under legal obligation to protect a woman who is in danger by prompt and clear action. In other places they are not obliged to do anything. When the laws are not specific, every police officer is free to decide. Some police officers understand domestic violence and some do not. Those who have been involved in working with women's shelters quickly understand the desperate situation in which battered women find themselves and can be genuinely helpful. In any case, the police won't beat her or kill her.

A battered woman often forgets that even though she is in trouble, she is still a citizen of the United States and is entitled to be protected by law. Although the laws in various parts of the country are different, she will find that in most places the police will ask if she is willing to file charges against the man who is battering her. She should say yes.

And she should do it.

It may be the best thing she can do for both of them. It will be better for him than allowing him to continue his violent behavior. It may force him into a program that can help him stop battering. It may help him find a way to deal with his anger in more acceptable ways. If it doesn't help him, at least it will make him stop hitting her. It will certainly be better for her than allowing him to continue using her as a punching bag.

Victims of family violence, professional family violence counselors who deal with these problems every day, judges, and law enforcement officers agree that an important way to stop battering is to let the batterer know that his actions will have consequences. If he doesn't understand this, he has no incentive to change his ways. If he's not interested in changing, there's no way he can be helped. But at least he will stop hitting her.

As discussed in Chapter 8, most states provide legal recourse for battered women. Restraining orders and protective orders can prevent the batterer from harassing her, going near her home or workplace, or attempting to communicate with her or her children. The police will know how to find additional help. They may help her go to a safe place to stay with friends or family members. Representatives from the local family crisis center can come to the police station to take her to the family shelter. If the nearest shelter is full, they will try to find a place for her in another town if necessary.

What If No One Believes Her?

Suppose she has found the courage to tell her doctor or lawyer or clergyperson or some other advisor what her partner has been doing to her and the person she tells insists that her story is unreasonable or that she is crazy or that her partner would never do such awful things. She should remind this professional person that their conversation is confidential and that professional ethics forbid mentioning her problem outside the office. That should protect her from violent retribution by her partner, but it won't help her. What is she going to do?

Suppose she tells a friend or relative or associate and that person also refuses to believe her. What is she going to do?

She should try to remember that her story does sound unbelievable. After all, if she had believed her partner capable of doing such things, she would never have gotten involved with him. She should remember that batterers are manipulative and devious. She should remember that he has such a Jekyll and Hyde personality that he can even fool her.

Once she has told someone who doesn't believe her, she can be sure that person is going to tell her partner about the conversation. And when that happens, she is in real danger.

Battered Women's Shelters

She should immediately find the battered women's shelter nearest her and go to it. Shelters for battered women are not exclusively for poor women. They are there for every woman who needs the special help they offer.

If she can't find the shelter in her community, she must find some other safe place where she can spend the night. If she can't find any other safe place, she should call the police and ask them to take her to the nearest battered women's shelter because her husband is trying to kill her.

Planning Ahead

If she is not in acute danger at the moment, it would be a good idea to plan ahead for a time when she will be. She should decide what she will take with her if and when she actually decides to leave the battering relationship.

If she wants custody of her children, she should be prepared to take them with her when she leaves. She may need to pick them up from school or from after-school activities, and to do so she may need a good excuse. She must be ready to do what she has to do to protect them and to protect her right to custody of them.

She shouldn't be ashamed to talk to friends or relatives who may be willing to shelter her, even if it is only temporary. A woman who is contemplating escape from a battering situation must find a way to let her friends or relatives know about her situation so that they won't be surprised when she suddenly arrives on their doorstep. If she can't force herself to ask for help, she might tell them a story about a make-believe person who might someday need this sort of help and listen carefully to what they say. Or she could drop hints they can't help but understand. They may already suspect or even know what has been happening to her, and be waiting for her to ask for help.

If she has a friend or relative she can completely trust not to turn her possessions over to her abusive partner, she might manage to "accidentally" leave a change of clothing and some personal belongings at their house. If there is absolutely no one near her whom she can trust, she might rent a locker at a bus station or airport and keep her belongings there. Or she might ask the people at the battered women's shelter to help her find a safe storage place.

To make her great escape back to the world of sense and sanity, she will need access to important personal papers such as birth certificates, immunization records, passports, social security cards, and wedding and baptismal records.

She should make an inventory of all separately and jointly held assets, including investments, cars, and furniture. It may be necessary for her to have this inventory, along with a list of outstanding debts, to determine a fair division of property.

It would also be helpful for her to have copies of her income tax returns, deeds to property, car registrations and titles, statements from savings or checking accounts, stocks, bonds, mutual fund certificates, and any other papers that show her ownership rights to money or property.

If she can't take these papers with her without arousing the batterer's suspicion, she might be able to make photocopies of them while he is away from the house. The public library, the post office, and some schools have coin-operated copy machines. She should keep these papers or copies in a safe place.

If there is no safe place in her home, she should leave them with the friends she has trusted with her clothes. If she has no friends she can completely trust, she can rent a safety deposit box at a bank, in her name alone, so nobody else will have access to its contents. If she can't rent a safety deposit box, she can leave her papers in the locker she rented at the bus station or airport. Or she can rent a post office box and mail the papers to herself.

If the battered woman and her partner already have a joint safety deposit box, she should have the bank verify its contents before she leaves.

Money is going to be a *big* problem when she leaves, so she should try to save some in a secret bank account or hiding place. This will give her some ready cash and a small measure of control over her life. Since she has no privacy, saving is of course hard.

If her partner finds the money she is saving, she can tell him she was saving it to buy a special gift for his birthday, their anniversary, or some other occasion. Then she must buy him something with part of the money.

If she is still free to go out of the house alone, she should check with the credit departments of any stores at which they have joint charge accounts or she has charge accounts in her own name. Batterers often charge large purchases and seldom pay the bills. They also hide the mail so the battered woman does not know that outstanding bills are ruining her credit.

To protect her personal credit, she should close any accounts to which the batterer has access. If she wishes to keep them open, she should notify the creditors in writing that she will no longer be responsible for her spouse's purchases. Sometimes the stores will agree to close the accounts by making it appear that this was the store's decision, without mentioning the fact that this action was at her request.

If she discovers that their joint accounts are charged with small unpaid bills, she should try to pay them or encourage her partner to pay them. If they are charged with large unpaid bills, she should discuss the matter with the store manager. She can explain that her partner is responsible for payment. Stores can sometimes force him to pay.

If she hopes to receive child support or alimony, she must keep a careful list of her monthly and yearly expenses so that her attorney can present a credible case if she should decide on a divorce.

What Happens When She Calls a Shelter?

The first question the shelter staff usually asks is, "Are you in danger at this moment?"

If she is in trouble or in danger when she calls them, she shouldn't be ashamed to tell them. If she is hurt and bleeding alone in a telephone booth somewhere in the dark, she can tell them. They've heard it all before. They won't be shocked. They will find a way to help her. If she is not in acute danger when she calls them, they can help her keep from getting into that situation.

Crisis intervention services, family crisis centers and women's shelters can provide temporary emergency shelter for a woman and her children if it is needed. In this safe house her privacy and needs will be respected, her partner cannot reach her, and she is out of danger. Its location is never made public. The shelter staff can even arrange for someone to meet her and take her to the safe house. If she or her children are hurt, they will arrange for emergency medical treatment. If she escaped with nothing but the clothes on her back, as many women and children do, they can even provide a change of clothes.

If a woman is in serious danger and her life has been threatened, she may prefer to go to a shelter that is far away from her batterer. For example, if her family lives in another city, the shelter can find a way to send her to that city.

While she is in the shelter the battered woman will be in a controlled environment where she can begin to recover some of the resources which the batterer has stolen from her.

She will be able to start breathing freely and thinking for herself.

Legal Help

The people at the crisis center know that battered women usually don't have money for lawyers. In an attempt to meet this need, many centers and shelters are in contact with lawyers who can help a woman take advantage of her right to protection under the law.

They can help her apply for restraining orders or protective orders so that her abusive partner will not be able to continue to threaten her. If her partner has managed to get her into trouble with the law, savvy lawyers can sometimes help her find ways to make restitution or otherwise get out of the trouble she is in. Some judges are beginning to understand the terrible effects of domestic violence, and when an advocate from the family crisis center accompanies a woman to court, she will receive a fair and sympathetic hearing.

If a woman is severely battered or mutilated when she escapes, she can ask a staff member to take photographs of her injuries to use as evidence in future legal battles such as a divorce or custody case. The photographs should have a date and the name of the person who took them written on them.

How Long Will She Stay at the Shelter?

The average woman stays in a shelter from one to six weeks, although sometimes a person needs to stay a little longer. While she is in the shelter or the counseling program, the woman will receive help in the form of education about her rights and counseling about how to redirect her life. She will be asked to think about her goals and decide what she wants to accomplish, both while she is there and when she leaves. The shelter staff will help her understand the options that are open to her.

How Will Her Partner Respond?

At some time while she is in the shelter or the counseling program, the battered woman can expect her partner to attempt to contact her. If he should find his way to the shelter, the staff will speak with him, but they won't let him in and they won't let him see her or her children unless she agrees. If he telephones the shelter, the staff will take his number and give her the message. She should be prepared. He will show his charming side and try to make her want to go home.

If she decides not to see him, she shouldn't be surprised if he enlists the aid of his friends, his family, her family, or even his clergyman to plead his case. These people may attempt to visit her at the shelter. The shelter staff will not let them near her unless she agrees. If they telephone the shelter, the staff will take their numbers and give her the messages. She is not obliged to return any of their calls.

If the woman does agree to see them or talk to them, they will usually tell her how sad her partner is, how difficult it is for him to get along without her, how much he loves her, how much he misses her, and how much he needs her. All these things may be perfectly true, but this time, she needs to think about herself: how she feels, whether she is sad or relieved, how she is getting along, and what she needs.

These visitors will almost certainly try to make her feel guilty. They may tell her that she is responsible for all her troubles, that the beatings she suffered were not so bad, that a woman "has to take the bad with the good." They may try to force her to return to the batterer, or they may try to encourage her to see him.

She can listen to them if she wants to, but she doesn't have to. And she certainly doesn't have to do what they say. She is not responsible for her troubles or she would have stopped them. The beatings she suffered were bad, and they are no small problem. She doesn't have to take the bad with the good when the bad includes battering. She is not making a big thing out of a small problem. And she doesn't have to do anything she doesn't want to do.

If she has children, her husband may insist on visiting them. The shelter staff can arrange a controlled environment where he will not be able to harm them or to kidnap them. She can ask a staff member to be there during the entire visit to be sure the children are safe. If she agrees to be there while he is visiting the children, she shouldn't be surprised to find him ignoring the children and spending his time trying to make her feel guilty and bad about herself, or trying to get her back under his control.

He may even send her flowers or gifts at the shelter. She can keep them or refuse them. She can display them in the shelter for everyone to enjoy, or have them sent to a nursing home where they will bring a little joy to other people. She is in control of her life. She can make her own choices, without allowing the gifts to affect her decision.

Her partner or the people he sends to see her may try to tell her "Everything was just fine between you until you went to the shelter and those bad people put ideas into your head." Everything was not fine, or she wouldn't be in pain, in debt, in legal trouble, or in this situation.

It may be true that the counselors, advocates, and staff at the shelter are putting ideas into her head.

There's the idea that she doesn't deserve to be beaten.

There's the idea that she's a worthwhile person.

There's the idea that she is a capable, competent, and intelligent adult.

There's the idea that she can think for herself.

There's the idea that she can do things for herself.

There's the idea that she should be free to come and go as she pleases.

There's the idea that she should be able to visit with friends and relatives when she wishes to do so.

There's the idea that she has the right to live a life that is free of violence and abuse.

These are not such bad ideas. Some of them may have been in her head all along, just waiting until she was safe enough to think them.

Can the Batterer Change?

Where there's life there's always hope. Programs such as Alcoholics Anonymous and Weight Watchers have proved that anyone who sincerely wants to change can. Unfortunately, not all battering men are interested in changing.

Those men who have recently turned to battering as a reaction to uncontrollable forces in their life, such as a job loss, a demotion at work, severe stress, or health problems, and who feel terrible about what they are doing or becoming can often be helped.

There is little hope for real change in those men who grew up in violent homes, who are involved in a long-term battering relationship, or who enjoy their lives exactly as they are and do not want to change.

In spite of what battered women may have been told, family crisis centers and women's shelters are not in the business of breaking up families. They are in the business of saving lives. Many of them provide counseling services for the batterers. Others can direct the batterers to places where they can get counseling, if they want to turn their lives around.

Counselors and Support Groups at the Shelter

While she is in the shelter, counselors will help the battered woman set important goals. They will advise her on what she can do to help herself after she leaves the shelter. They will discuss her special problems with her and help her find a way to solve them. They will help her find medical or legal help, look for a place to live, find a job, or apply for financial aid or food stamps.

While she is in the shelter, she may decide she wants to find a job or find a way to get job training so that she can earn a better living. She may decide to arrange for a permanent separation. She may decide to file for divorce or she may want to find a place to live. She may want to try marriage counseling with her partner while she is living in a safe place.

Most family crisis centers and women's shelters also have long-term support groups where she will learn to understand her situation, express her feelings, and regain her self-esteem. Some centers and shelters also offer counseling and support groups for the children of abused families. Some even provide family counseling to help the abusive men and any other family members affected by family violence.

If she is not in immediate danger, has a secure place to stay, or doesn't want to leave the battering situation yet, she doesn't have to move into the shelter to be helped. They offer outreach services including individual one-on-one counseling and support groups.

In many shelters, walk-in counseling programs are available for battered women who don't need to stay at the shelter, as are after-care programs for women who now live without their abusive partners. These programs may help meet her needs for long-term support, child care, job assistance, and affordable housing.

Support groups are completely confidential, and they are on a first name basis. The other women in the groups are, or have been, in the same situation.

Family centers have found that one of the best ways to help a battered woman is through the support of small groups of five or seven women who will provide her with on-going support, care, and understanding. These groups will help build her confidence, bolster her self-esteem, and show her techniques for dealing with the abusive man. If she has felt unique in her suffering, she will find women in these groups who understand exactly what she has been going through.

Some groups meet once a week for as long as twelve weeks. Other groups are "open groups," which also meet once a week and will welcome the battered woman with support anytime she appears. They are important to the woman whose situation makes it impossible for her to attend a regular weekly meeting.

Fees for attending these groups are normally calculated on a sliding scale, based on the woman's income, if she has any income. Such things as how many children she has, her debts, and her costs of living are considered and, if her circumstances change during the twelve weeks, her fees can be renegotiated.

Suppose the battered woman has stayed in the shelter or been in the counseling program in the past. Or suppose she has been helped by the police or a family crisis center in the past and she has returned to the battering relationship. Suppose she has made a mistake and finds herself in danger again. She should not be ashamed to call for help.

She is not the only person in the world who has found herself in this situation. While some determined women are able to break free the first time they leave the battering relationship, many others go back as many as three or four times before they are able to start their lives over again.

She can do it, too.

Today.

10

Who To Call for Help

YOU'RE FEELING HELPLESS, BLACK
AND BLUE, DESPERATE, AND
TRAPPED—OR KNOW SOMEONE
WHO IS

Her Safety First

The violence will not simply stop, and it will not get better. Once it starts it will happen more often and it will get progressively worse. No matter how much a battered woman loves her partner, she should know that she is in real danger. She has to ensure her own safety.

Jim Mattox, the former Attorney General of Texas, put the matter in perspective when he said, "Family violence is a serious problem in Texas and across the country. Protecting yourself and your children from violence, or the threat of violence, is the first concern in such situations."

To obtain that protection, she must take the first step. She must gather her courage together and call for help. She can call a friend, her family, or the police. She can call her church, a physician, or a counselor. She can call the women's center, women's shelter, or family crisis center nearest her.

Battered women's centers, crisis intervention services, and family crisis centers have names like Council for Abused Families, Coalition Against Domestic Violence, Crisis Intervention Service, or Family Help Place. Family crisis centers provide hotlines that are open twenty-four hours a day, seven days a week.

If she cannot find the family crisis center, she can call the police, sheriff, district attorney, public library, or Salvation Army. The Salvation Army has kind and caring people who will help her without regard to her color, religion, or ethnic background. They can put her in touch with the people who can give her exactly the help she needs.

A battered woman must not stop until she finds that help. Her life depends on it.

IF SHE KNOWS SHE NEEDS HELP BUT SHE DOESN'T EVEN KNOW WHAT KIND OF HELP SHE'S GOING TO NEED:

She can call the police department or look in the phone book under the heading of crisis intervention services to get the number for the nearest family crisis center or domestic violence center.

To receive information about domestic violence and referral to local shelters from anywhere in the continental USA, call:

National Coalition Against Domestic Violence,
(303) 839-1852

National Victim Center, 1-800-FYI-CALL

The following state-by-state listing does not include all the shelters or intervention and prevention programs available in the nation, but if she calls one of the numbers, they will refer her to the shelter nearest her.*

Alabama
Birmingham: Crisis Center, (205) 323-7777
   Safe House of Shelby County, (205) 644-4357
Dothan: House of Ruth, (205) 793-2232 or (205) 793-7784
   (sexual assault)
Florence: Safeplace Crisis Line, (205) 767-6210 or
   (205) 767-6392
Mobile: Penelope House Crisis Line, (205) 342-8994
Montgomery: Domestic Abuse Shelter, (205) 263-0218; Safe Place
   for Teens, (205) 265-2652

---

*Phone numbers were viable at the time of publication; the author and publisher are not responsible for number changes or discontinued programs.

Alaska

Anchorage: Abused Women's Aid in Crisis, (907) 272-0100 or
(907) 279-9581
Alaska Women's Resource Center, (907) 276-0528
Standing Together Against Rape (STAR), (907) 563-7273 or
(907) 563-9981
Bethel: Tundra Women's Coalition, (907) 543-3456
Dillingham: Safe & Fear-Free Environment, (907) 842-2316 or
(907) 842-2320
Emmonak: Emmonak Women's Shelter, (907) 949-1434
Fairbanks: Women in Crisis Counseling & Assistance,
(907) 452-RAPE or (907) 452-2293
Homer: South Peninsula Women's Services, (907) 235-7712
Juneau: Aiding Women in Abuse & Rape Emergencies (AWARE),
(907) 586-1090 or (907) 586-6623
Child Care & Family Resources, (907) 586-3785
Tongass Community Counseling Center, (907) 586-3585
Kenai: Leeshore Women's Resource & Crisis Center,
(907) 283-7257 or (907) 283-9479
Ketchikan: Women in Safe Homes, (907) 225-9474
Kodiak: Kodiak Women's Resource & Crisis Center,
(907) 486-3625 or (907) 486-6171
Kotzebue: Maniilaq's Women's Crisis Program, (907) 442-3969
Nome: Bering Sea Women's Group, 1-800-570-5444
Palmer: Valley Women's Resource Center, 1-800-478-4090 or
(907) 376-4080
Seward: Seward Life Action Council, (907) 224-3027
Sitka: Sitkans Against Family Violence, 1-800-478-6511 or
(907) 747-6511
Unalaska: Unalaskans Against Sexual Assault & Family Violence,
1-800-478-7238, (907) 581-1500, or (907) 581-3310
Valdez: Advocates for Victims of Violence, (907) 835-2999 or
(907) 835-2980

Arizona

Campe Verde: Verde Valley Guidance Clinic, (602) 567-4026
Casa Grande: Against Abuse, Inc., (602) 836-0858
Cottonwood: Verde Valley Guidance Clinic, (602) 634-2236
Flagstaff: Flagstaff Battered Women's Shelter, (602) 774-4503
Glendale: Faith House, (602) 939-6798
Mesa: Autumn House, (602) 835-5555

Nogales: Family Guidance Center, (602) 281-9009 or
(602) 287-4713
Phoenix: De Colores (Valle Del Sol), (602) 269-1515
Sojourner Center, (602) 258-5344
Salvation Army, (602) 267-4130
Prescott: Faith House, (602) 445-4673
Safford: Domestic Violence in Graham/Greenlee County,
(602) 428-4550
Sedona: Verde Valley Guidance Clinic, (602) 282-HELP
Sierra Vista: Domestic Crisis Shelter, (602) 458-9096
Tempe: Arizona Coalition Against Domestic Violence,
(602) 279-2900
Tucson: AVA Crisis Shelter, (602) 795-4880
Brewster Crisis Shelter Services, (602) 622-6347
Tucson Center, (602) 795-4266
Whiteriver: Apache Behavioral Health Services, (602) 338-4811
Yuma: Safe House, (602) 782-0044

Arkansas
Arkadelphia: Abused Women & Children, 1-800-246-2587 or
(501) 246-3122
Camden: Women's Crisis Center, (501) 836-0325
Fayetteville: Project for Victims of Family Violence,
(501) 442-9811
Fort Smith: Women's Crisis Center, (501) 782-4956
Harrison: Sanctuary, (501) 741-2121
Little Rock: Advocates for Battered Women, (501) 376-3219 or
(501) 376-3221
Pine Bluff: Women's Shelter, (501) 535-0287 or (501) 535-2955
Texarkana: Domestic Violence Prevention, Inc., (903) 793-4357
or (903) 794-4000

California (North and Central)
Auburn: Placer Women's Center, (916) 823-4185 or
(916) 885-0443
Berkeley: Emergency Shelter, (510) 786-1246
Chico: Catalyst, (916) 895-8476
Concord: Battered Women's Alternatives, (510) 930-8300
Davis: Sexual Assault & Domestic Violence Center,
(916) 662-1133
El Dorado: El Dorado Women's Information Center, (916) 626-1131

Who to Call for Help

Eureka: Humboldt Women for Shelter, (707) 444-9255
Fairfield: Solano Center for Battered Women, (707) 429-4357
Fremont: SAVE (Shelter Against Violent Environments),
    (510) 794-6055 or (510) 794-6056
French Camp: Haven of Peace, (209) 982-0396
Fresno: YWCA Marjaree Mason Center, (209) 237-4701
Gilroy: Discover Alternatives, (408) 683-4118
Grass Valley: Domestic Violence & Sexual Assault Coalition,
    (916) 272-3467
Hayward: Emergency Shelter Program, (510) 581-5626
Lakeport: AWARE Inc./Agape House, (707) 263-1133
Livermore: Tri-Valley Haven for Women, (510) 449-5842
Madera: Shelter and Help in Emergency, (209) 673-8776
Modesto: Haven/Stanislaus Women's Refuge, (209) 577-5980
Monterey: YWCA Domestic Violence Program, (408) 372-6300
Mountain View: Support Network, (415) 940-7855
Napa: NEWS (Napa Emergency Women's Service),
    (707) 255-6397 or (707) 252-3687
Newark: Second Chance Emergency Shelter, (510) 792-4357
Oakland: A Safe Place, (510) 536-SAFE or (510) 444-7255
Pine Grove: Operation Care, (209) 223-2600
Placerville: El Dorado Women's Information Center,
    (916) 626-1131
Porterville: Porterville Mission Project Women's Shelter,
    (209) 784-0192
Reading: Shasta County Women's Refuge, (916) 244-0117
Sacramento: WEAVE, Inc., (916) 920-2952
Salinas: Shelter Plus, 1-800-339-8228 or (408) 422-2201
San Andreas: Calaveras Women's Crisis Line, (209) 736-4011
San Francisco: La Casa de las Madres, (415) 333-1515 or
    (415) 777-1808
    WOMAN, Inc., (415) 864-4722
    Family Violence Project, (415) 252-8900
San Jose: Next Door, (408) 279-2962
San Luis Obispo: Women's Shelter Program, 1-800-549-8989
    or (805) 544-3494
San Mateo: Northern California Shelter Support Services,
    (415) 342-0850
San Rafael: Marin Abused Women Services, (415) 924-6616
Santa Cruz: Women's Crisis Support and Shelter Service,
    (408) 429-1478

Santa Rosa: YWCA Women's Emergency Shelter, (707) 546-7115
or (707) 546-1234
Selma: Good Samaritan Mission, Inc., (209) 896-9927
Sonora: Mother Lode Women's Crisis Center, (209) 532-4707
South Lake Tahoe: Womenspace Unlimited, (916) 544-4444
Stockton: DAWN (Directions for Abused Women in Need),
(209) 465-4878
Ukiah: Project Sanctuary, (707) 462-9196 or (707) 462-7862
Visalia: Battered Women's Shelter, 1-800-448-2044 or
(209) 732-5941
Yuba City: Casa de Esperanza, (916) 674-2040 or (916) 664-5400

California (Southern)

Artesia: Su Casa Family Crisis and Support, (310) 402-4888 or
(310) 402-7081
Bakersfield: Alliance on Family Violence, 1-800-273-7713 or
(805) 327-1091
Canoga Park: Haven Hills, (818) 887-6589
Claremont: House of Ruth, (909) 988-5559
Colton: Option House, Inc., (909) 381-3471
El Centro: Woman Haven, (619) 353-8530
Glendale: Glendale YWCA Shelter for Women, (818) 242-1106 or
(818) 242-1107
Hanford: Domestic Violence Prevention Program, 1-800-540-5433
Lancaster: Valley Oasis, (805) 945-6736
Lompoc: Shelter Services for Women, (805) 736-0965
Long Beach: YWCA Women's Shelter, (310) 437-4663
Los Angeles: Good Shepherd Shelter, 8-10 P.M. only,
(213) 737-6111
Center for the Pacific Asian Family, 1-800-339-3940 or
(213) 653-4042
Chicana Service Action Center, (213) 268-7564
Jenesse Center, 1-800-479-7328 or (213) 751-1145
Newbury Park: Interface Community, 1-800-339-9597
North Hollywood: Shiloh, (818) 776-9789
Orange: Women's Transitional Living Center, (714) 992-1931
Pasadena: Haven House, (213) 681-2626
Riverside: Horizon House, 1-800-339-SAFE or (909) 683-0829
San Diego: Battered Women's Services, (619) 234-3164
Domestic Violence INFOLINE, (619) 683-2500 twenty-four
hours, in English and Spanish

Battered Women's Casa de Paz, (619) 239-2342
Interfaith Shelter Network, (619) 563-0771
San Luis Rey: Women's Resource Center, (619) 757-3500
San Pedro: Rainbow Shelter, (310) 547-9343
Santa Barbara: Shelter Services for Women, (805) 964-5245
Santa Monica: Sojourn, (310) 392-9896 or (310) 399-9239
Twenty-Nine Palms: Unity Home, (619) 366-9663
Ventura: Ventura County Coalition Against Household Violence,
    (805) 656-1111
Victorville: High Desert Domestic Violence, (619) 242-9179
West Covina: YWCA Helpline, (818) 967-0658

Colorado
Alamosa: Tu Casa, Inc., (719) 589-2465
Arvada: Women in Crisis, (303) 420-6752
Aspen: Response, (303) 925-SAFE
Aurora: Gateway Battered Women's Shelter, (303) 343-1851
Boulder: Boulder County Safehouse, (303) 444-2424
Commerce City: Alternatives to Family Violence, (303) 289-4441
Canon City: Family Crisis Service, (719) 275-2429
Craig: Abused and Battered Humans, (303) 824-2400
Denver: Safehouse for Battered Women, (303) 830-6800
    Brandon Center, (303) 620-9190
Durango: Alternative Horizons, (303) 247-9619
Ft. Collins: Crossroads, (303) 482-3502
Ft. Morgan: SHARE, (303) 867-3411
Frisco: Advocates for Victims of Assault, (303) 668-3906
Glenwood Springs: Advocates Safehouse Project, (303) 945-4439
    or (303) 945-2632
Grand Junction: Domestic Violence Project, (303) 241-6704
Greeley: A Woman's Place, (303) 356-I-CAN
Leadville: Advocates of Lake County, (719) 486-3530
Longmont: Longmont Coalition for Women in Crisis,
    (303) 772-4422
Loveland: Alternatives for Battered Women, (303) 663-2288
Montrose: Women's Resource Center, (303) 249-2486
Pueblo: YWCA Family Crisis Shelter, (719) 545-8195
Steamboat Springs: Advocates Against Battering and Abuse,
    (303) 879-8888
Vail: Women's Resource Center of Eagle County, (303) 476-7384

Connecticut
Ansonia: The Umbrella, (203) 736-9944
Bridgeport: YWCA Shelter Services for Abused Women, (203) 334-6154
Danbury: Domestic Violence Hotline, (203) 731-5206
Danielson: Battered Women's Program, (203) 774-8648
Falls Village: Women's Emergency Services, (203) 824-1080
Greenwich: Domestic Abuse Service (YWCA), a part of the Safe Home Network, (203) 622-0003
Hartford: Connecticut Coalition Against Domestic Violence, (203) 524-5890
Hartford Interval House, (203) 527-0550 or (203) 246-9149
Meriden: Meriden-Wallingford Chrysalis, (203) 238-1501 or (203) 237-3713
Middletown: New Horizons, (203) 347-6971
New Britain: Prudence Crandall Center, (203) 225-6357
New Haven: Domestic Violence Services of Greater New Haven, (203) 789-8104 or (203) 865-1957
New London: Genesis House, (203) 447-0366
Norwalk: Women's Crisis Center, a member of the Safe Home Network, (203) 852-1980
Stamford: Domestic Violence Services (YWCA), (203) 357-8162
Torrington: Susan B. Anthony Project for Women, (203) 482-7133
Waterbury: Women's Emergency Shelter, (203) 575-0036

Delaware
New Castle County: CHILD, Inc., (302) 762-6110
Kent and Sussex Counties: People's Place II/Families in Transition, (302) 422-8058
Wilmington: Delaware Commission for Women, Department of Community Education, (302) 577-2660

District of Columbia
My Sister's Place, (202) 529-5991

Florida
Statewide Hotline: 1-800-342-9152
Bartow: Peace River Center, (813) 682-7270
Bradenton: HOPE Family Services, Inc., (813) 747-8499
Clearwater: Spouse Abuse Shelter, (813) 442-4128
Dade County: Safespace, Dade County Advocates; north side shelter, (305) 758-2546; south side shelter, (305) 247-4249

Daytona Beach: Domestic Abuse Council, (904) 255-2102
Ft. Lauderdale: Women in Distress, (305) 761-1133 or
 (305) 760-9800
Ft. Myers: ACT, (813) 939-3112
Gainesville: SPARC, 1-800-393-SAFE or (904) 377-8255
Jacksonville: Hubbard House, (904) 354-3114
Key West: Domestic Abuse Shelter, (305) 294-0824,
 (305) 743-4440, or (305) 852-6222
Kissimmee: Help NOW, (407) 847-8811
Miami: see Dade County
Naples: Shelter for Abused Women of Collier County,
 (813) 775-1101
Ocala: Rape Crisis/Spouse Abuse Center, (904) 622-8495
Orlando: Spouse Abuse, 1-800-892-2849, (407) 886-2856, or
 (407) 886-2244
Pensacola: Favorhouse, (904) 434-6600 or (904) 434-1177
Port Richey: Salvation Army Shelter, (813) 856-5797
Sarasota: Safe Place and Rape Crisis Center, (813) 365-1976
St. Petersburg: Center Against Spouse Abuse, (813) 898-3671
Tallahassee: Refuge House, (904) 681-2111
Tampa: The Spring, (813) 247-7233
West Palm Beach: Domestic Assault Project, (407) 355-2383
 YWCA Domestic Assault Shelter, (407) 655-6106

Georgia
Albany: Liberty House, (912) 439-7065 or (912) 439-7094
Atlanta: Atlanta Council on Battered Women, (404) 873-1766
Augusta: Safe Homes of Augusta, (706) 736-2499
Brunswick: Amity House, (912) 264-4357
Gainesville: Gateway House, Inc., (404) 536-5860
Hinesville: Coastal Area Community Mental Health,
 (912) 368-HELP
Jonesboro: Clayton County Association of Battered Women, Inc.,
 (404) 996-HELP or (404) 961-7233
Macon: Crisis Line, (912) 745-9292
Marietta: Crisis Intervention Line (YWCA), (404) 427-3390
Rome: Hospitality House for Women, (706) 235-4673
Savannah: SAFE Shelter, Georgia Network Against Domestic
 Violence, (912) 234-9999
Waycross: Shelter for Abused Women and Children/The Shelter,
 (912) 285-5850

Hawaii
Hawaii: Family Crisis Shelter, (808) 959-5825
Kauai: YWCA—The Shelter, (808) 245-6362
Maui: Women Helping Women, (808) 579-9581
Molokai: Alternatives to Violence, (808) 553-3202
   Hale Ho'omalu, shelter for battered women, (808) 567-6888
Oahu: Shelter for Abused Spouses and Children, (808) 841-0822

Idaho
American Falls: Domestic Violence Support Group,
   (208) 226-2311
Blackfoot: Bingham Crisis Center for Women, (208) 785-3811
Boise: Women's Crisis Center, (208) 343-7025
   Idaho Council on Family Violence, (208) 334-6512
Coeur d'Alene: Women's Center, (208) 664-1443
Idaho Falls: Domestic Violence Intervention Center,
   (208) 529-4352
Lewiston: Sue Wheel Richmond (YWCA) Shelter, (208) 746-9655
Moscow: Alternatives to Violence, University of Idaho,
   (208) 883-4357
Nampa: Mercy House (YWCA), (208) 465-5011
Pocatello: Women's Advocates (YWCA), (208) 235-2503
Twin Falls: Volunteers Against Violence, (208) 733-0100
Wallace: Women's Resource Center, dial 911 or call
   (208) 556-6101 or (208) 556-1114

Illinois
Statewide Hotline: 1-800-252-6561
Alton: Oasis Women's Center, (618) 465-1978
Aurora: Mutual Ground, (708) 897-0080
Belleville: Women's Crisis Shelter, (618) 235-0892
   PAVE, (618) 533-SAFE
Bloomington: Neville House, (309) 827-7070
Cairo: Women's Shelter, (618) 734-HELP
Canton: Women's Crisis Service, (309) 647-8311
Carbondale: Women's Center, 1-800-334-2094 or (618) 529-2324
Charleston: Coalition Against Domestic Violence,
   (217) 345-4300 or (217) 235-4300
Chicago: Abused Women's Coalition, (312) 278-4566
   Department of Human Services, (312) 744-8418

Family Rescue, (312) 375-8400
Rainbow House/Arco Iris, (312) 521-4865
Southwest Women Working Together, (312) 582-0550
Women Abuse Action Project, Hull House, (312) 561-3500
Women's Services, Loop YMCA, (312) 372-6600 ext. 265
Danville: YWCA Women's Shelter, (217) 443-5566 or
    (217) 443-5568
Decatur: DOVE, (217) 423-2238
De Kalb: Safe Passage, (815) 756-2228
Des Plaines: Life Span, (708) 824-4454
Elgin: Community Crisis Center, (708) 697-2380
Evanston: YWCA, (708) 864-8780
Freeport: YWCA, (815) 235-1641
Glen Ellyn: Family Shelter Service, (708) 469-5650
Harrisburg: Anna Bixby Women's Center, 1-800-421-8456 or
    (618) 252-8389
Hazelcrest: South Suburban Family Shelter, (708) 335-3028
Jacksonville: Women's Crisis Center, (217) 243-HELP
Joliet: Groundwork, (815) 729-1228
Kankakee: Coalition Against Domestic Violence, (815) 932-5800
La Grange: Domestic Violence Hotline, (708) 485-5254
Oak Park: Sarah's Inn, (708) 386-4225
Peoria: Center for Prevention of Abuse, (309) 691-4111 or
    (309) 691-0551
Princeton: Quad Counties Counseling Center, (815) 875-4458
Quincy: Network Against Domestic Abuse, (217) 222-2873
Rochelle: HOPE, (815) 562-8890
Rockford: WAVE, (815) 962-6102
Springfield: Sojourn Shelter & Service, (217) 544-2484
Sterling: COVE (YWCA), (815) 626-7277
Streator: Alternatives to Domestic Violence, 1-800-892-3375
    or (815) 673-1555
Urbana: A Woman's Place, (217) 384-4390
Waukegan: A Safe Place/Lake County Crisis Center,
    (708) 249-4450
Woodstock: Turning Point, 1-800-892-8900

Indiana
Anderson: Women's Alternatives, (317) 643-0200
Bloomington: Middle Way House, Inc., (812) 333-7404
Columbus: Turning Point, (812) 379-9844

Crawfordsville: Family Crisis Center of Montgomery County, (317) 362-2030
Evansville: Albion Fellows Bacon Center, (812) 422-5622
 YWCA Shelter, (812) 422-1191
Ft. Wayne: YWCA Women's Shelter, (219) 447-7233
Gary: Commission on the Status of Women, (219) 883-4155
Hammond: Haven House, (219) 931-2090
Hobart: The Caring Place, 1-800-933-0466
Indianapolis: Salvation Army Family Service, (317) 637-5551
 Sojourner, (317) 635-4674
Kokomo: Family Intervention Center, (317) 459-0314
Lafayette: YWCA Women's Shelter, (317) 423-1118
Marion: Women's Services, (317) 664-0701
Michigan City: The Stepping Stone, 1-800-248-1151 or (219) 879-4615
Muncie: A Better Way, (317) 747-9107
New Albany: YWCA Spouse Abuse Center, (812) 944-3839
Richmond: Genesis, (317) 935-3920
South Bend: YWCA Women's Shelter, (219) 232-9558
Terre Haute: Council on Domestic Abuse, (812) 232-1736

Iowa

Statewide Hotlines: 1-800-383-2988 or 1-800-942-0333
Ames: ACCESS, 1-800-203-3488
Burlington: DOVES (YWCA), (319) 752-4475
Cedar Falls/Waterloo: Integrated Crisis Service, (319) 233-8484
Cedar Rapids: YWCA Women's Shelter, (319) 363-2093
Clinton: YWCA Women's Resource Center, (319) 242-2118
Council Bluffs: Domestic Violence Program, (712) 328-0266
Davenport: Domestic Violence Advocacy Program, (319) 326-9191
 in Scott County and (319) 797-1777 in Rock Island
Decorah: Services for Abused Women, 1-800-383-2988
Des Moines: Coalition Against Domestic Violence, (515) 281-7284
 Sexual Assault Care Center, (515) 288-1750
Dubuque: YWCA Battered Women Program, (319) 556-1100
Ft. Dodge: Domestic/Sexual Assault Outreach Center, (515) 573-8000
Iowa City: Domestic Violence Project, (319) 351-1043
 Iowa City Shelter Program, 1-800-373-1043

Mason City: Crisis Intervention Service, (515) 424-9133
Marshalltown: Domestic Violence Alternatives, (515) 753-3513
Muscatine: Domestic Abuse/Sexual Assault Advocacy Program, (319) 263-8080
Ottumwa: The Crisis Center and Women's Shelter, 1-800-464-8340 or (515) 683-3122
Sioux City: Council on Sexual Assault and Domestic Violence, 1-800-982-7233 or (712) 258-7233

Kansas
Atchison: Atchison Social and Rehabilitation Services, (913) 367-5345 ext. 243
DOVES, Inc., 1-800-367-7075 or (913) 367-0363
Concordia: Domestic Violence Task Force, (913) 243-3131
Dodge City: Domestic Violence Hotline, (316) 225-6510
Emporia: SOS, 1-800-825-1295 or (316) 342-1870
Garden City: Family Crisis Service, (316) 275-5911
Great Bend: Family Crisis Center, (316) 792-1885
Hays: Northwest Kansas Family Shelter, 1-800-794-4624 or (913) 625-4202
Hutchinson: Coalition Against Spouse Assault, (316) 663-2522
Kansas City: Women's Transitional Care, (913) 843-3333
Leavenworth: Alliance Against Family Violence, (913) 682-1752
Manhattan: Crisis Center, Inc., 1-800-727-2785 or (913) 539-2785
Parsons/Pittsburg: Safehouse, 1-800-794-9148 or (316) 231-8251
Salina: Domestic Violence Association of Central Kansas, 1-800-874-1499 or (913) 827-5862
Topeka: Battered Women Task Force, (913) 233-1730 or (913) 354-7927
Wichita: YWCA Women's Crisis Center, (316) 267-SAFE

Kentucky
Statewide Crisis Line: (502) 581-7222; seven days, 24 hours; will accept collect calls
Ashland: Safe Harbor, 1-800-926-2105 or (606) 329-9304
Beattyville: Resurrection Home, (606) 464-8481
Bowling Green: Brass, (502) 843-1183
Covington: Women's Crisis Center, (606) 491-3335
Elizabethtown: Helping Hand, (502) 769-3092

Hazard: Women and Children's Safe House, 1-800-928-3131 or (606) 439-5129

Hopkinsville: Sanctuary, (502) 885-4572

Lexington: YWCA Spouse Abuse Center, (606) 255-9808

Louisville: Seven Counties Services Crisis and Information Center, 1-800-221-0446 or (502) 589-4313

Madisonville: Sanctuary, (502) 825-9737

Maysville: Women's Crisis Center, (606) 564-6708 or 1-800-928-6708

Newport: Women's Crisis Center, (606) 491-3335

Owensboro: Owensboro Area Spouse Abuse and Information Services, (502) 685-0260

Paducah: Purchase Area Spouse Abuse Center, 1-800-585-2686 or (502) 443-6001

Somerset: Bethany House, 1-800-755-2017 or (606) 679-8852

Louisiana

Alexandria: Family Counseling/Battered Women's Program, (318) 448-0284

Baton Rouge: Capitol Area Family Violence Intervention Center, 1-800-541-9706 or (504) 389-3001

Hammond: Southeast Spouse Abuse Program, 1-800-256-1143 or (504) 542-8384

Lake Charles: Calcasieu Women's Shelter, (318) 436-4552

Mandeville: Safe Harbor (YWCA), (504) 624-4939

New Iberia: Safety Net for Abused Persons, (318) 367-7627

New Orleans: Project Save, (504) 523-3755 ext. 2923
YWCA Battered Women's Program, (504) 486-0377 or (504) 482-9922 (daytime only)

Shreveport: Family Crisis Center, (318) 221-0933

Slidell: Safe Harbor (YWCA), (504) 643-9407

Maine

Auburn: Abused Women's Advocacy Program, (207) 795-4020

Augusta: Maine Coalition for Family Crisis Services, Family Violence Assistance Project, (207) 623-3569

Bangor: Spruce Run Associates, (207) 947-0496

Dover-Foxcroft: Womancare, (207) 564-8165 or (207) 564-8401 after hours

Machias: Womankind, (207) 255-4785

Portland: Family Crisis Shelter, 1-800-537-6066
Presque Isle: Family Support Center, (207) 769-8251
Rockland: New Hope for Women, (207) 236-4867
Saco: Caring Unlimited, York County Domestic Violence Center,
(207) 282-2182

Maryland

Allegany County: Family Crisis Resource Center, Inc.,
(301) 759-9244 or (301) 759-9246
Annapolis: Maryland Network Against Domestic Violence (YWCA
Women's Center), (410) 757-8300 daytime or (410) 222-7273
after hours
Baltimore City: House of Ruth, (410) 889-7884 or
(410) 385-2263
Baltimore County: Family Crisis Center, (410) 285-4357
Sexual Assault/Domestic Violence Center, (410) 391-2396 or
(410) 828-6390
Carroll County: Battered Spouse Program, (410) 857-0077
Easton: Mid-Shore Council on Family Violence, (410) 822-5276
Frederick County: Heartly House, (301) 662-8800
Garrett County: House of Hope, (301) 334-2357
Hartford County: Sexual Assault/Spouse Abuse Resource Center,
(410) 836-8430 or (410) 879-3486
Howard County: Domestic Violence Center of Howard County,
(410) 997-2272
Montgomery County: Abused Persons Program, (301) 654-1881
Prince Georges County: Family Crisis Center, (301) 864-9101
Washington County: CASA/New Directions for Women,
(301) 739-4990

Massachusetts

Boston: Casa Myrna Vazquez, (617) 521-0100
Elizabeth Stone House, (617) 522-3417
Harbor Me, (617) 889-2111
Massachusetts Coalition of Battered Women's Service
Groups and Jane Doe Safety Fund, (617) 248-0922
Renewal House, (617) 566-6881
Brockton: A Womansplace, (508) 588-2041
Cambridge: Transition House, (617) 661-7203
Fitchburg: Women's Resources, (508) 342-9355, (508) 630-1031,
or (508) 368-1311

Greenfield: New England Learning Center for Women in
Transition, (413) 772-0806
Holyoke: Womanshelter/Companeras, (413) 536-1628
Hyannis: Independence House, 1-800-439-6507 or (508) 771-6507
Lawrence: Women's Resource Center, (508) 685-2480
Lowell: Alternative House, (508) 458-0274
New Bedford: New Bedford Women's Center, (508) 999-6636
Northampton: Necessities, (413) 586-5066
Somerville: Respond, (617) 623-5900
Springfield: HERA (Hotline to End Rape and Abuse),
(413) 732-3456
Waltham: Waltham Battered Women's Support Committee,
(617) 899-8676
Worcester: Daybreak, (508) 755-9030
Abby's House, (508) 756-5486

Michigan
Michigan Upper-Peninsula Hotline: 1-800-956-6656
Alpena: Shelter, (517) 356-9650
Ann Arbor: SAFE House, (313) 995-5444
Assault Crisis Center, (313) 483-7273
Battle Creek: Safe Place, (616) 965-7233
Bay City: Bay County Women's Center, (517) 686-4551
Benton Harbor: The Shelter, (616) 983-4275
Cadillac: OASIS, (616) 775-7233
Calumet: Barbar Kettle Gundlach Shelter Home for Abused
Women, (906) 337-5623
Coldwater: Shelter House, (517) 278-7432
Detroit: Interim House (YWCA), (313) 861-5300
Escanaba: Delta County Spouse Abuse Program, (906) 428-2121
Flint: SAFE House of Flint, (810) 238-SAFE
Grand Haven: Center for Women-In-Transition, (616) 842-HELP
or (616) 458-HELP
Grand Rapids: YWCA Domestic Crisis Center, (616) 451-2744 or
(616) 744-3535
Hart: Domestic Violence & Sexual Assault, 1-800-950-5808
Hillsdale: Domestic Harmony, (517) 439-1454
Howell: La Casa, (810) 227-7100
Huntington Woods: Michigan Coalition Against Domestic
Violence, (810) 857-8078
Ionia: Spouse Abuse Center, Eight Cap, Inc., 1-800-720-SAFE
or (616) 527-3351

Iron Mountain: Caring House, 1-800-232-3226 or (906) 774-1112

Ironwood: Domestic Violence Escape, (906) 932-4990

Jackson: AWARE Shelter, (517) 783-2671

Kalamazoo: Domestic Assault Program (YWCA), (616) 385-3587

Lansing: Council Against Domestic Assault, (517) 372-5572

Marquette: Harbor House, 1-800-455-6611, (906) 226-2791, or
(906) 226-6611

Midland: Council on Domestic Violence, (517) 835-6771

Mt. Clemens: Turning Point, (810) 463-6990

Mt. Pleasant: Domestic Violence Project Women's Aid Service,
(517) 772-9168

Muskegon: Spouse Assault Crisis Center, 1-800-950-5808
Everywoman's Place, (616) 722-3333

Petoskey: Women's Resource Center Safe Home, (616) 347-0082

Pontiac: HAVEN, (810) 334-1274

Port Huron: Domestic Assault & Rape Elimination Services,
(810) 985-5538

Saginaw: Underground Railroad, (517) 755-0411

Sault Ste. Marie: Domestic Violence Program, (906) 635-0566

Traverse City: Women's Resource Center, (616) 941-1210

Minnesota

Statewide Hotline: (612) 646-0994

Belle Plaine: Southern Valley Battered Women's Alliance,
(612) 873-4214

Bemidji: Northwoods Coalition for Battered Women,
(218) 751-0211

Brainerd: Women's Center of Mid-Minnesota, (218) 828-1216

Chisolm: Range Women's Advocates, 1-800-232-1300

Circle Pines: Alexandra House, (612) 780-2330

Duluth: Domestic Abuse Intervention Project, (218) 722-4134
Women's Coalition, (218) 728-6481

Eagan: B. Robert Lewis House, (612) 452-7288

Fergus Falls: Women's Crisis Center, (218) 739-3359

Hopkins: Sojourner Shelter, (612) 933-7422

International Falls: Friends Against Abuse, (218) 285-7220

Lake Elam: Family Violence Network, (612) 770-0777

Mankato: Commission Against Domestic Abuse, (507) 532-2350

Marshall: Southwest Women's Shelter, (507) 532-2350

McGregor: Mid-Minnesota Women's Center, (218) 828-1216

Minneapolis: Harriet Tubman Shelter, (612) 827-2841
Indian Health Board Family Violence Program, (612) 721-9800

Domestic Abuse Project, (612) 874-7063
Plymouth: Home Free Shelter, (612) 559-4945
Rochester: Women's Shelter, (507) 285-1010
St. Cloud: Woman House, (612) 252-1603
St. Paul: Casa de Esperanza, (612) 772-1723
Minnesota Coalition for Battered Women, (612) 646-0994 or (612) 646-6177
Women of Nations, (612) 222-5830
Woman's Advocates, (612) 227-8284
Thief River Falls: Violence Intervention Project, (218) 681-5557
Two Harbors: North Shore Horizon, (218) 834-5924
Willmar: Shelter House, 1-800-476-3234 or (612) 231-9154
Winona: Women's Resource Center, Battered Women's Task Force, (507) 452-4440

Mississippi
Biloxi: Gulf Coast Women's Center, (601) 435-1968
Mississippi Coalition Against Domestic Violence, (601) 435-1968
Columbus: SAFE HAVEN, c/o Golden Triangle Medical Center, (601) 327-6040 or (601) 327-6118
Jackson: Shelter for Battered Families, c/o Catholic Charities, (601) 362-9782
Laurel/Hattiesburg: Domestic Abuse Family Shelter, (601) 428-8821
Meridian: Care Lodge, (601) 693-HOPE (4673)
Oxford: Domestic Violence Project, 1-800-227-5764 or (601) 234-5085
Tupelo: SAFE, (601) 841-2273 or 1-800-527-7233

Missouri
Colombia: The Shelter, (314) 875-1369 or 1-800-548-2480
Fulton: SERVE, (314) 642-6388
Independence: Hope House, (816) 461-4673
Jefferson City: RACS, (314) 634-8346 or (314) 634-4911
Joplin: Family Self-Help Center, (417) 782-1772
Kansas City: NEWS House, (816) 241-0311
Rose Brooks, (816) 861-6100
St. Charles: Women's Center, (314) 946-6854
St. Joseph: YWCA, (816) 232-1225 or (816) 232-4481

St. Louis: ALIVE, Inc., (314) 993-2777
Missouri Coalition Against Domestic Violence, Women's
Self-Help Center, (314) 531-2003
St. Martha's Shelter, (314) 533-1313
Sedalia: CASA, (816) 827-5555
Springfield: Family Violence Center, (417) 865-1728
Warrensburg: Survival, (816) 429-2847
Waynesville: Pulaski County Crisis Center, (314) 774-2628

Montana

Billings: Montana Coalition Against Domestic Violence,
(406) 256-6334
YWCA Gateway House, (406) 259-8100 or (406) 245-4472
Bozeman: Battered Women's Network, (406) 586-4111
Chester: Help for Abused Spouses, (406) 759-5170
Dillon: Women's Resource Center, (406) 683-6106
Glendive: Task Force Against Spouse Abuse, (406) 365-6477
Great Falls: Mercy Home, (406) 453-1018
Helena: Friendship Center, (406) 442-6800
Kalispell: Rape Crisis Line, (406) 752-7273
Libby: Women's Help Line, (406) 293-3223
Miles City: Clark St. Inn, (406) 232-1688
Missoula: YWCA Domestic Violence Assistance Center,
(406) 542-1944
Women's Place, (406) 543-7606
Pablo: Family Crisis Center, (406) 676-2518
Twin Bridges: Madison County Unit Against Spouse Abuse,
(406) 843-5301 or (406) 842-5454

Nebraska

Bellevue: Family Service, 1-800-523-3666
Women Against Violence Crisis Line, YWCA, (402) 345-7273
Benkelman: Domestic Violence Task Force, 1-800-607-1497 or
(308) 423-2676
Broken Bow: Domestic Abuse Task Force, 1-800-942-4040 or
(308) 872-5988
Columbus: Center for Survivors, (402) 564-2155
Crete: Coordinated Intervention System for Domestic Abuse,
(402) 826-2332
Fremont: Domestic Abuse Program, (402) 727-7777 or
(402) 721-4340

Gordon: Family Rescue Shelter, (308) 282-0126
Grand Island: Crisis Center, (308) 381-0555
Hastings: Spouse Abuse Crisis Center, (402) 463-4677
Kearney: SAFE Center, (308) 237-2599
Lexington: Parent/Child Center, (308) 324-3040
Lincoln: Friendship Home, (402) 475-7273 or (402) 474-4709
  Rape/Spouse Abuse Crisis Center, (402) 475-7273 or
  (402) 476-2110
McCook: Domestic Abuse Services, (308) 345-5534
Norfolk: Bright Horizons, (402) 379-3798
North Platte: Rape and Domestic Abuse Program, (308) 534-3495
  or (308) 532-0624
Omaha: The Shelter, (402) 558-5700
  Women Against Violence (YWCA), (402) 345-7273
Scottsbluff: Domestic Violence Task Force, (308) 436-HELP
Wayne: Haven House Family Services Center, 1-800-440-4633 or
  (402) 375-4633

Nevada
Statewide Hotline: 1-800-500-1556
Carson City: Advocates to End Domestic Violence,
  (702) 883-7654
Ely: Support Inc., (702) 289-2270 or (702) 289-8808
  after hours
Fallon: Domestic Violence Intervention, (702) 423-3116
Las Vegas: Temporary Assistance for Domestic Crisis,
  (702) 646-4981
Minden: Family Support Council, (702) 782-8692
Sparks: Committee to Aid Abused Women, (702) 358-4150
  Nevada Network Against Domestic Violence, 1-800-500-1556
  or (702) 358-4214
Reno: Advocates to End Domestic Violence, (702) 883-7654
  Community Counseling and Suicide Prevention, 1-800-992-5757
  or (702) 323-6111 (crisis lines); (702) 323-4533 (office)
Yerington: ALIVE, Domestic Violence Crisis Lines,
  1-800-453-4009 or (702) 463-4009

New Hampshire
Berlin: Berlin Task Force on Family Violence, Coos County
  Family Health Services, 1-800-852-3388 or (603) 752-2040
Claremont: Women's Supportive Services, (603) 543-0155

Concord: New Hampshire Coalition Against Domestic and Sexual
  Violence, 1-800-852-3388 or (603) 224-8893
Conway: Carroll County Against Domestic Violence and Rape,
  1-800-336-3795 or (603) 356-7993
Keene: Women's Crisis Service of the Monadnock Region,
  (603) 352-3782
Laconia: New Beginnings, 1-800-852-3388 or (603) 528-6511
Lebanon: WISE, (603) 448-5525 or (603) 448-5922
Littleton: Support Center Against Domestic Violence and Sexual
  Assault, 1-800-774-0544 or TDD, 1-800-RELAY-NH
Manchester: Women's Crisis Service (YWCA), (603) 668-2299
Nashua: Rape and Assault Support Services, (603) 883-3044
Plymouth: Plymouth Area Task Force Against Domestic Violence,
  (603) 536-1659
Portsmouth: A Safe Place, 1-800-852-3388 or (603) 436-7924

New Jersey
Statewide Hotline: 1-800-572-SAFE
Atlantic County: Atlantic County Women's Center,
  1-800-286-4184 or (609) 646-6767
Bergen County: Shelter Our Sisters, Hackensack, (201) 944-9600
  Alternatives to Domestic Violence, Hackensack,
  (201) 487-8484
Burlington County: Providence House, Burlington,
  (609) 871-7551
Camden County: Solace, (609) 227-1234
Cape May County: Coalition Against Rape and Abuse,
  (609) 522-6489
Cumberland County: Cumberland County Women's Center,
  (609) 691-3713
Essex County: Family Violence Project, Newark, (201) 484-4446
  The Safe House, (201) 759-2154
Gloucester County: People Against Spouse Abuse, County Health
  Center, Woodbury, (609) 848-5557 (outreach office) or
  (609) 881-3335 (shelter & hotline)
Hudson County: Battered Women's Program (YWCA), Jersey City,
  (201) 333-5700
Hunterdon County: Women's Crisis Services, Flemington,
  (908) 788-4044 or (908) 788-7666
Mercer County: Womanspace, Trenton, (609) 394-9000
Middlesex County: Women Aware, Inc., (908) 249-4504

Monmouth County: Women's Center of Monmouth County, Hazlet, (908) 264-4111

Morris County: Jersey Battered Women Service, Morristown, (201) 267-4763 or (201) 455-1256

Ocean County: Providence House, 1-800-246-8910 or (908) 244-8259 (also TTD)

Passaic County: Women's Center, (201) 881-1450

Salem County: Salem County Women's Services, (609) 935-6655, also a TDD number; FAX number, (609) 935-6165

Somerset County: Resource Center for Women, Somerville, (908) 685-1122

Sussex County: Domestic Abuse Services, Inc., (201) 875-1211

Union County: Battered Women's Project (YWCA), Elizabeth, (908) 355-4357, (908) 355-1995, or (908) 355-1996

Warren County: Domestic Abuse and Rape Crisis Center, Belvedere, (908) 453-4181

New Mexico
Alamorgordo: COPE, (505) 437-2673

Albuquerque: The Women's Community Association, (505) 247-4219

Clovis: Shelter for Victims of Domestic Violence, 1-800-401-0305, (505) 762-0050, or (505) 769-0305

Farmington: Family Crisis Center, (505) 325-3549

Gallup: Battered Families, (505) 722-7483

Hobbs: Option Inc., (505) 397-1576

Laguna: Laguna Family Services, 1-800-530-2199

Las Cruces: La Casa, Inc., 1-800-376-2272, (505) 526-2819, or (505) 526-9513 (shelter)

Roswell: The Refuge, (505) 624-0666

Santa Fe: Esperanza, (505) 473-5200

Silver City: El Refugio, (505) 538-2125

Taos: Community Against Sexual and Domestic Violence, (505) 758-9888 or (505) 758-8082

New York
Statewide Hotline: 1-800-942-6906

Albany County: Comprehensive Crime Victims Assistance Program, (518) 447-5500 (24 hours) or (518) 445-7735 (days only)

Broome County: SOS Shelter, (607) 754-4340
  YWCA Interfaith Service, Binghamton, (607) 772-0340

Cattaraugus County: Domestic and Rape Crisis Hotline,

(716) 945-3970
Haven House, Buffalo, (716) 884-6000
Chataugue County: YWCA-Alternatives to Violence, Jamestown, (716) 488-2237
Domestic Violence Hotline, (716) 484-0052
Chemung County: American Red Cross, Elmira, (607) 734-3317
Victims of Domestic Violence, Salvation Army, (607) 732-1979
Chenango County: Catholic Charities, Norwich, (607) 336-1101
Clinton County: Stop Domestic Violence, (518) 563-6904
Cortland County: SOS Shelter, (607) 754-4340
Aid to Women Victims of Violence (YWCA), Cortland, (607) 756-6363
Delaware County: Safe Against Violence, (607) 746-6278
Duchess County: Grace Smith House, (914) 471-3033
YWCA of Duchess County, (914) 485-5550 or (914) 454-6770
Erie County: Haven House, (716) 884-6000
Essex County: Stop Domestic Violence, (518) 563-6904
Greene County: Greene County DSS, (518) 943-3200
Jefferson County: Women's Center Inc., (315) 782-1855 or (315) 782-1823
Madison County: Victims of Violence, c/o Liberty Resources, (315) 366-5000 or (315) 363-0048
Monroe County: Alternatives for Battered Women, Inc., Rochester, (716) 232-7353
Montgomery County: Task Force for Battered Women, (518) 842-3384
Nassau County: Coalition Against Domestic Violence, (516) 542-0404
New York City (Brooklyn): Park Slope Safe Homes Project, (718) 499-2151
Women's Survival Space, (718) 439-7281
New York City (Manhattan): Henry St. Settlement Shelter, (212) 475-6400
Niagara County: Family & Children's Services, (716) 285-6984
Lockport YWCA, (716) 433-6714
YWCA of the Tonawandas, (716) 692-5643
Haven House, (716) 884-6000
Onondaga County: Syracuse YWCA, (315) 424-0040
Abused Person's Unit, (315) 425-2111
Ontario County: Three County Domestic Violence Task Force, Geneva, (315) 789-2613
Family Counseling Services, (914) 561-0301

Orleans County: Department of Social Services, (716) 589-7004

Ostego County: Aid to Battered Women, (607) 432-4855 or
(607) 433-8320

Rensselaer County: Unity House, Families in Crisis,
(518) 272-2370

Rockland County: Rockland Family Shelter, (914) 425-0112

Schenectady County: Battered Women's Shelter (YWCA),
(518) 374-3386

Schuyler County: Task Force for Battered Women, (607) 277-5000

Suffolk County: Long Island Women's Coalition, Southside
Hospital, (516) 666-8833

Tioga County: Victim Assistance Center of Tioga County (VAC),
Owego, (607) 687-6866

Tompkins County: Task Force for Battered Women, Ithaca,
(607) 277-5000

Ulster County: Family Adult Shelter, (914) 338-2370 or
(914) 679-2485

Westchester County: Shelter, N. Westchester, (914) 747-0707

North Carolina

Alamance County: Domestic Violence and Child Abuse Services,
(910) 226-5985

Burke County: Options, Inc., (704) 438-9444

Caldwell County: Shelter Home, Lenoir, (704) 758-0888

Cabarras County: Victims Assistance Network, (704) 788-2826

Chatham County: HELP LINE, (919) 929-0479

Cherokee County: REACH, (704) 837-8064 (weekdays) or
(704) 837-7477

Craven County: Task Force on Domestic Violence, (919) 638-5995

Cumberland County: Care Center, Fayetteville, (910) 323-4187

Davidson County: Domestic Violence Services, Lexington,
(704) 249-8974

Forsyth County: Battered Women's Services, Winston-Salem,
(910) 723-8125

Gaston County: Battered Spouse Program, (704) 867-4357 or
(704) 866-3613

Guilford County: Women's Shelter, High Point, (910) 841-8255
North Carolina Association of Domestic Violence Programs,
(910) 841-8255
Family and Children's Service, (910) 333-6910 (weekdays) or
(910) 274-7316

High Point: North Carolina Association of Domestic Violence
Programs, High Point Women's Shelter, (910) 841-8255
Mecklenburg and Union Counties: The Shelter, Charlotte,
(704) 332-2513
Nash and Edgecombe Counties: My Sister's House,
(919) 977-2892
New Hanover County: Domestic Abuse Shelter, Wilmington,
(910) 343-0703
Orange County: Orange-Durham Coalition for Battered Women,
(919) 489-1955
Pasquotank County: Albemarle Hopeline, (919) 338-3011
Rockingham County: HELP, Inc., (910) 342-3331
Rowan County: Family Abuse Crisis Council, (704) 636-9222
Wake County: Family Violence Prevention, (919) 571-4954
Watauga County: OASIS, (704) 262-5035
Wayne County: Shelter of Wayne, (919) 736-1313
Wilkes County: SAFE, (910) 667-7656
Wilson County: Wesley Shelter, (919) 291-2344

North Dakota
Statewide Hotline: 1-800-472-2911
Bismarck: Abused Adult Resource Center, (701) 222-8370
North Dakota Council on Abused Women's Services, State
Networking Office, (701) 255-6240
Bottineau: Coalition Against Domestic Violence, (701) 228-3171
Devil's Lake: Safe Alternatives for Abused Families,
(701) 662-7378
Dickinson: Domestic Violence and Rape Crisis Center,
(701) 225-4506
Fargo: Rape and Abuse Crisis Center, (701) 293-7273
Ft. Berthold Reservation: Coalition Against Domestic Violence,
(701) 627-3653
Grand Forks: Abuse and Rape Crisis Center, (701) 746-8900
Jamestown: SAFE, (701) 251-2300
McLean County: McLean's Family Resource Center,
(701) 462-8643
Mercer County: Women's Action and Resource Center, Beulan,
(701) 873-2274 (days) or (701) 748-2274 (nights)
Minot: Domestic Violence Crisis Center, (701) 852-2258
Williston: Family Crisis Shelter, (701) 572-9111 or
(701) 572-0757

THE BATTERED WOMAN'S SURVIVAL GUIDE

Ohio

Akron: Battered Women's Shelter, (216) 374-0740

Alliance: Alliance Area Domestic Violence, (216) 823-7223

Ashtebula: Homesafe, (216) 992-2727

Athens: My Sister's Place, (614) 593-3402

Batavia: House of Peace (YWCA), (513) 753-7281

Bellefontaine: CHOICES, (614) 224-4663

Canton: Domestic Violence Project, (216) 453-SAFE

Celina: Family Crisis Network, (419) 586-1133

Chardon: Women Safe, (216) 564-9555

Chillicothe: Crisis Center, (614) 773-4357
   Domestic Violence Task Force, (614) 775-5396 (days only)

Cincinnati: Alice Paul House, (513) 241-2757

Cleveland: Templum House, (216) 631-2275

Columbus: CHOICES, (614) 224-4663
   Action for Battered Women in Ohio, (614) 221-1255

Dayton: YWCA Battered Women's Project, (513) 222-6333

Defiance: Northwestern Ohio Crisis Line, (419) 782-1100

Eaton: Preble County Counseling Center, (513) 456-6201

Findlay: Council on Domestic Violence, (419) 422-4766

Fostoria: Domestic Violence Shelter, 1-800-466-6228 or
   (419) 435-7300

Hamilton: Shelter for Battered Persons and Their Children
   (YWCA), (513) 863-7099

Highland County: Domestic Violence Task Force, 1-800-339-5066
   or (513) 393-8118 (days only)

Hillsboro: Domestic Violence Task Force, (513) 393-9904

Lancaster: Lighthouse, (614) 687-4423

Lebanon: Family Abuse Shelter, (513) 932-6301
   Warren County Crisis Counseling Center, 1-800-932-3366

Lima: Crossroads Crisis Center, (419) 228-4357

Mansfield: The Shelter, (419) 526-4450

Marietta: EVE, Inc., (614) 374-5819

Marion: Turning Point, (614) 382-8988

Mt. Vernon: New Directions, (614) 397-4357

Newark: New Beginnings, (614) 345-4498

Painesville: Forbes House, (216) 953-9779

Portsmouth: Southern Ohio Task Force on Domestic Violence,
   (614) 354-1010 or (614) 456-8217 (days only)

Reedsville: Serenity House, (614) 446-5554

St. Clairsville: Women's Tri-County Help Center, (614) 695-5441

Sidney: New Choices, (513) 498-7261
Springfield: Project Woman, (513) 325-3707
Toledo: Battered Women Shelter (YWCA), (419) 241-7386
Troy: Family Abuse Shelter, (513) 339-6761
Van Wert: Crisis Care Line, (419) 238-4357
Warren: Someplace Safe, (216) 393-1565
Waverly: Service & Assistance for Victims of Spousal Abuse,
    (614) 947-2147
Wooster: Everywoman's House, (216) 263-1020
Xenia: Domestic Violence Project, (513) 372-4552
Youngstown: Sojourner House, (216) 747-4040
Zanesville: Transitions, (614) 454-3214
    Response, (614) 454-6001

Oklahoma
Statewide Hotline: 1-800-522-7233
Ada: Services for Battered Women, (405) 436-3504
Altus: ACMI House, (405) 482-3800
Bartlesville: Women and Children in Crisis, (918) 336-1188
Chickasha: Women's Service Center, 1-800-734-4117 or
    (405) 222-1818
Clinton: ACTION Assoc., (405) 323-2604 or (405) 323-0838
Enid: Option House (YWCA), (405) 234-7644
Lawton: New Directions, (405) 357-2500 or (405) 357-6141
Miami: Community Crisis Center, (918) 542-1001
Muskogee, Tahlequa: Help in Crisis (HIC), (918) 456-4357
Norman: Norman Shelter for Battered Women, (405) 360-0590
Oklahoma City: YWCA Crisis Intervention Services,
    (405) 949-1866 or (405) 947-4506
Stillwater: Stillwater Domestic Violence Services,
    (405) 624-3020 or (405) 624-3028
Talequah: Help in Crisis, Inc., 1-800-300-5321 or
    (918) 456-HELP
Tulsa: Domestic Violence Intervention Services, (918) 585-3143
Woodward: Northwest Domestic Violence Services, (405) 256-8712

Oregon
Ashland: Dunn House, (503) 779-HELP
Astoria: Women's Crisis Service, (503) 325-5735
Bend: COBRA, 1-800-356-2369, (503) 389-7021, or
    (503) 382-9227

Corvallis: Center Against Rape and Domestic Violence,
(503) 754-0110

Eugene: Womenspace, (503) 485-6513 or (503) 485-8232
Family Shelter Home, (503) 689-7156

Grants Pass: Women's Crisis Support Team, 1-800-750-9278,
(503) 474-1400, or (503) 479-9349

Hines: HOPE, (503) 573-7176

Hood River: Helping Hands Against Violence Project,
(503) 386-6603

Klamath Falls: Klamath Crisis Center, (503) 884-0390

La Grande: Shelter from the Storm, (503) 963-9261 or
(503) 963-7226

Lakeview: Crisis Intervention Center, 1-800-338-7590

Lincoln City: Lincoln Shelter and Services, 1-800-841-8325 or
(503) 994-5959

McMinnville: Henderson House, (503) 472-1503

North Bend: Women's Crisis Service, 1-800-448-8125,
(503) 756-7000, or (503) 756-7864

Ontario: Project DOVE, (503) 889-2000

Oregon City: Clackamas Women's Service, (503) 654-2288

Pendleton: Awakening House, 1-800-833-1161 or (503) 278-0241

Portland: Bradley-Angle House, (503) 281-2442
Portland Women's Crisis Line, (503) 235-5333 or
(503) 232-9751

Roseburg: Battered Persons' Advocacy Project, (503) 673-6641
or (503) 673-7867 (after hours)

St. Helens: Women's Resource Center, (503) 397-6161

Salem: Midvalley Women's Crisis Center, (503) 378-1572

The Dalles: Haven from Domestic Violence, (503) 298-4789

Tillamook: Crisis and Resource Center, 1-800-992-1679 or
(503) 842-9486

Washington County: Shelter/Domestic Violence Resource Center,
(503) 640-1171

Pennsylvania

Allentown: Turning Point, (215) 437-3369

Beaver: Women's Center, (412) 775-0131

Bloomsburg: Women's Center, 1-800-544-8293 or
(717) 784-6631

Chambersburg: WIN Victims' Services, (717) 264-4444

Doylestown: A Woman's Place, 1-800-220-8116

Erie: Hospitality House Services for Women, (814) 454-8161
Greensburg: Women's Services of Westmoreland County,
(412) 836-1122 or (412) 836-9540
Harrisburg: Battered Women's Shelter, 1-800-654-1211
Pennsylvania Coalition Against Domestic Violence
(Note: not a hotline number; avail. weekdays only),
1-800-932-4632 in Penn., 1-800-537-2238 outside Penn.
Johnstown: Women's Help Center (YWCA), 1-800-999-7406 or
(814) 536-5361
Lancaster: Women Against Abuse, (717) 299-1249
Lewisburg: Women in Transition, 1-800-850-7948 or
(717) 374-7773
McKeesport: Womansplace, (412) 678-4616
Meadville: Women's Services, (814) 333-9766 or (814) 724-4637
Media: Domestic Abuse Project, (215) 565-4590
New Castle: Women's Shelter, (412) 652-9036
Norristown: Laurel House, (215) 643-3150 or (215) 885-5020
Philadelphia: Women Against Abuse, (215) 386-7777
Pittsburgh: Women's Center and Shelter, (412) 687-8005
Reading: Berks County Women in Crisis, (215) 372-9540
Sharon: AWARE, (412) 981-1457
Stroudsburg: Women's Resource Center, (717) 421-4200
Tarentum: HOPE Center, part of the Safe Home Network,
(412) 339-4673
Towanda: Women's Center, part of the Safe Home Network,
(717) 265-9101
Union City: Horizon House, (814) 438-2675
Warren: Women's Center, 1-800-338-3460, (814) 726-1030,
or (814) 726-1271
Wilkes-Barre: Domestic Violence Service Center, (717) 823-7312
or (717) 823-5834
Zelienople: Volunteers Against Abuse Center, 1-800-400-8551 or
(412) 776-6790

Rhode Island
Central Falls: Rhode Island Council on Domestic Violence,
(401) 723-3051
Newport: Newport County Women's Resource Center,
(401) 847-2533
Providence: Sojourner House, (401) 658-4334 or (401) 861-6191
Women's Center, (401) 861-2760

Warwick: Elizabeth Buffum Chase House, (401) 738-1700
Wyoming: Women's Resource Center of South County,
   (401) 847-2533

South Carolina
Aiken: Aiken Help Line, (803) 648-9900
Columbia: Sistercare, (803) 765-9428
   South Carolina Coalition Against Domestic Violence and Sexual
   Assault, (803) 254-3699 or (803) 771-7273 (rape crisis line)
Conway: CASA, (803) 248-7376
Greenville: Shelter, (803) 467-3636
   Family Counseling Center, (803) 467-3434
North Charleston: My Sister's House, (803) 744-3242
Rock Hill: Sister-Help, (803) 329-2800
Sumter: Sumter Safe House (YWCA), (803) 775-2763

South Dakota
Aberdeen: Resource Center for Women, (605) 226-1212
Brookings: Women's Shelter, (605) 692-7233
Hot Springs: Crisis Intervention Team, (605) 745-6070
Mission: White Buffalo Calf Society for Women, (605) 856-2317
Rapid City: Women and Violence, Inc., (605) 341-4808
Sioux City: Citizens Against Rape and Domestic Violence,
   (605) 334-6645 or (605) 339-0116 (days only)
Vermillion: Coalition Against Domestic Violence,
   (605) 624-5311
Watertown: Women's Resource Center, (605) 886-4300
Yankton: Yankton Task Force, (605) 665-4606

Tennessee
Alcoa: Haven House, (615) 982-1087
Bristol: The Shelter, (703) 466-2312
Chattanooga: Family and Children's Services, (615) 755-2822
Columbia: Crisis Response Line, (615) 381-4499
   Hope House, (615) 381-8580
Hickman County: Women Are Safe Shelter, (615) 729-3358
Johnson City: Salvation Army, (615) 926-2101
Kingsport: Contact Concern, (615) 246-2273
   Sullivan County Human Services Department, (615) 245-0171
Knoxville: Family Crisis Center, (615) 637-8000
Lawrence County: The Shelter, (615) 762-1115

Memphis: YWCA Shelter, (901) 458-1661
Morriston: CEASE, (615) 581-2220
Nashville: Crisis Center, (615) 244-7444
Newport: Safe Place, (615) 623-3125
Sullivan County: Sullivan County Human Services Dept.,
    (615) 245-0171

Texas

Abilene: Noah Project, 1-800-444-3551
Amarillo: Family Support Services—Rape Crisis/Domestic
    Violence Program, 1-800-749-9026
Angleton: Women's Center of Brazoria County, 1-800-243-5788
Arlington: The Women's Shelter, (817) 461-7949 (metro line) or
    (817) 460-5566
Austin: Center for Battered Women, (512) 928-9070
Bastrop: Family Crisis Center, (512) 303-7755
Bay City: Matagorda County Women's Crisis Center,
    1-800-451-9235 or (409) 245-9299
Baytown: Bay Area Women's Center, (713) 422-2292
Beaumont: Women & Children's Shelter of Southeast Texas,
    1-800-621-8882
Brownsville: Friendship of Women, Inc., (210) 544-7412
Bryan: Phoebe's Home, (409) 775-5355
Cleburne: Johnson County Family Crisis Center, 1-800-848-3206
Conroe (The Woodlands): Montgomery County Women's Center,
    (713) 292-4338, (713) 367-8003, or (409) 539-5757
Corpus Christi: Women's Shelter, 1-800-580-HURT or
    (512) 881-8888
Dallas: The Family Place, (214) 941-1991 or (214) 747-7467
    (SHOR program — provides temporary housing)
    Genesis Women's Shelter, (214) 942-2998 or (214) 559-2050
    (outreach program)
    Salvation Army Family Violence Shelter, (214) 688-4494,
    ext. 185
Del Rio: Amistad Family Violence & Rape Crisis Center,
    (210) 775-9612 or (210) 774-2744
Denton: Denton County Friends of the Family, 1-800-572-4031 or
    (817) 382-7273
Dumas: Safe Place, 1-800-753-7553 or (806) 935-2828
El Paso: Shelter for Battered Women, (915) 593-7300 or
    1-800-727-0511 or (915) 562-0077 (outreach program)

Ft. Worth: Women's Haven of Tarrant County, (817) 535-6464
Fredericksburg: Hill Country Community Needs Council,
    (210) 997-HELP
Galveston: Women's Resource & Crisis Center, (409) 765-SAFE
Gainesville: Cooke County Friends of the Family, Inc.,
    (817) 665-2873
Garland: New Beginning Center, (214) 276-0057
Grand Prairie: Brighter Tomorrows Inc., (214) 262-8383
Greenville: Women in Need, 1-800-7HELP-ME, (903) 454-HELP,
    or (903) 455-4612
Harlingen: Family Crisis Center, Inc., (210) 423-9304
Hondo: Medina County Family Life Center, (210) 426-5131
Houston: Houston Area Women's Center, 1-800-256-0551 or
    (713) 528-2121 (crisis lines); 1-800-256-0556 or
    (713) 528-5785 (counseling)
    The Roseate Women's Center of Northwest Houston,
    (713) 351-HELP
    Aid to Victims of Domestic Abuse (AVDA), (713) 224-9911
    Northwest Assistance Ministries' Family Violence Center,
    (713) 583-2539
Huntsville: Safe House (Walker County Family Violence
    Council), (409) 291-3369
Irving: New Tomorrows, (214) 438-6785
Jacksonville: Cherokee County Crisis Center Inc.,
    1-800-232-8519
Jourdanton: Atascosa Family Crisis Center, Inc.,
    (210) 769-HELP or (210) 769-2169
Kerrville: Hill Country Crisis Council, (210) 257-2400
Kilgore: Kilgore Community Crisis Center, 1-800-333-9148
    or (903) 984-2377
Killeen: Families in Crisis, (817) 634-8309
Laredo: Laredo Family Violence Center, (210) 727-7888
League City: Women's Resource & Crisis Center, (409) 332-4357
Longview: Women's Center of East Texas, Inc.,
    1-800-441-5555
Lubbock: Women's Protective Services, Lubbock, Inc.,
    1-800-736-6491 or (806) 747-6491
Marble Falls: Highland Lakes Family Crisis Center,
    (210) 693-5600 or (210) 693-3656
McAllen: Women Together/Mujeres Unidas, 1-800-580-4879 or

(210) 630-4878

Midland: Permian Basin Center for Battered Women and Their
Children, (915) 570-1465

Mineral Wells: Hope Inc., 1-800-585-1306

Nacogdoches: Women's Shelter of East Texas Inc.,
1-800-828-7233 or (409) 569-8850

New Braunfels: Comal County Women's Center, 1-800-434-8013,
(210) 620-HELP, or (210) 620-7520

Pampa: Tralee Crisis Center for Women, 1-800-658-2796

Paris: Family Haven Crisis & Resource Center, 1-800-444-2836
or (903) 784-6842

Pasadena: The Bridge Over Troubled Waters, (713) 473-2801

Perryton: Panhandle Crisis Center, 1-800-753-5308 or
(806) 435-5008

Plainview: Hale County Crisis Center, (806) 293-7273

Plano: Collin County Women's Shelter, (214) 422-7233

Richmond: Ft. Bend County Women's Center, (713) 342-4357

Round Rock: Williamson County Crisis Center, 1-800-460-7233 or
(512) 255-1212

San Angelo: ICD Family Shelter, 1-800-749-8631 or
(915) 655-5774

San Antonio: Battered Women's Shelter of Bexar County,
(210) 733-8810 or (210) 227-HELP

San Marcos: Hayes County Women's Center, (512) 396-4357

Santa Fe: HIS Ministries, (409) 925-4357

Seguin: Guadalupe County Women's Shelter, 1-800-834-2033 or
(210) 372-2780

Sherman: Crisis Center, (903) 893-5615

Stephenville: Cross Timbers Family Service, (817) 965-4357

Temple: Families in Crisis, (817) 773-7765

Texarkana: Domestic Violence Prevention, Inc.,
1-800-876-4808 or (903) 793-4357

Texas City: Women's Resource & Crisis Center, (409) 948-4357

Tyler: Crisis Center, 1-800-333-0358 or (903) 595-5591

Vernon: First Step, Inc., 1-800-657-9390 or (817) 553-4384

Victoria: Women's Crisis Center, (512) 573-4357

Waco: Family Abuse Center, 1-800-283-8401 or (817) 772-8999

Webster: Bay Area Turning Point, (713) 332-1683

Wichita Falls: First Step, Inc., 1-800-658-2683 or
(817) 692-1993

Utah

Ogden: Your Community Connection, (801) 394-9456

Provo: United Way Center for Women and Children in Crisis, (801) 377-5500

St. George: Safehouse, (801) 674-3950

Salt Lake City: YWCA, (801) 355-2804

Vermont

Bennington: Project to Advance Victims of Domestic Violence, (802) 442-2111

Brattleboro: Women's Crisis Center Shelter, (802) 257-7364 or (802) 254-6954

Burlington: Women Helping Battered Women Shelter, (802) 658-1996

Lebanon: WISE, (603) 448-5525 or (603) 448-5922

Montpelier: Central Vermont Shelter Project, (802) 223-0855

Morrisville: Clarina Howard Nichols Shelter, (802) 888-5256

Newport: ABATE ONE, (802) 334-6744

Rutland: Herstory House Shelter, (802) 775-3232

St. Johnsbury: Umbrella, (802) 748-8645

Springfield: New Beginnings, (802) 885-2050 or (802) 885-2368

Virginia

Statewide Hotline: 1-800-838-8238

Alexandria: Battered Women's Shelter, (703) 838-4911

Charlottesville: SHE (Shelter for Help in Emergency), (804) 293-8509 or (804) 293-6155

Culpepper: Services to Abused Families, Inc., (703) 825-8876 or (703) 349-0309 in the Fauquier County area

Danville: DOVES, (804) 791-1400

Dumfries: Turning Points, (703) 221-4951

Ft. Lee: Family Advocacy Program, (804) 765-2308

Fredericksburg: Council on Domestic Violence, (703) 373-9373

Hampton: Virginia Peninsula Council on Domestic Violence, (804) 723-7774

Lynchburg: Women's CARE, (804) 528-1041

Martainsville: Citizens Against Family Violence, (703) 632-8701

Norfolk: Women in Crisis (YWCA), (804) 625-5570

Norton: Hope House, 1-800-572-2278

Onacock: Coalition Against Domestic Violence (Eastern Shore), (804) 787-1329

Radford: Women's Resource Center, (703) 639-1123

Reston: Center for Community Mental Health, (703) 435-4940

Richmond: YWCA Women's Advocacy Program, (804) 643-0888
or (804) 796-3066

Staunton: Alternatives for Abused Adults, 1-800-56-HAVEN or
(703) 886-6800

Winchester: The Shelter, (703) 667-6466

Woodstock: Response, (703) 459-5161 or (703) 436-3136

Wytheville: Family Resource Center, (703) 228-8431

Washington

Statewide Hotline: 1-800-562-6025

Aberdeen: Domestic Violence Center of Grace Harbor,
(206) 538-0733

Bellevue: Eastside Domestic Violence Program, (206) 746-1940

Bellingham: Womancare Shelter, (206) 398-7606 or
(206) 734-3438
Domestic Violence Program, (206) 734-7271 or (206) 385-1485

Bremerton: ALIVE (YWCA), (206) 479-1980 or (206) 479-5118

Centralia/Chehalis: Human Responce Network, 1-800-244-7414
or (206) 748-6601

Ellensburg: Crisis Line, (509) 925-4168

Everett: Snohomish County Center For Battered Women,
(206) 252-2873

Forks: Services for Victims of Domestic Violence and Sexual
Assault, (206) 374-2273 or (206) 374-6611, office

Goldendale/ White Salmon: Counseling and Resource Center,
1-800-235-4765 or (509) 773-5801

Kent/Renton: DAWN, (206) 854-STOP

Longview: Emergency Support Shelter, (206) 636-8471 or
(206) 425-1176

Moses Lake: Crisis Line, (509) 765-1717

Mount Vernon: Battered Women's Project, (206) 336-9591

Newport: Family Crisis Network, (509) 447-5483 or
(509) 447-2274

Oak Harbor/ Whidbey Island: Citizens Against Domestic Abuse,
(206) 675-2232

Olympia: Safeplace, (206) 754-6300 or (206) 786-8754, office

Omak: The Support Center, (509) 826-3221

Port Angeles: Safe Home Domestic Violence Program,
(206) 452-4357

Port Townsend: Domestic Violence Program, (206) 385-5291

Pullman: Alternatives to Violence, (509) 332-4357
Republic: Community Services, (509) 775-3341
   Sheriff, (509) 775-3132
Richland: A Woman's Place, (509) 582-9841
Seattle: New Beginnings, (206) 522-9472
   Women's Resource Center, (206) 461-4882
   Catherine Booth House, (206) 324-4923
Spokane: Alternatives, (YWCA), (509) 327-9534
South Bend: Family Abuse Alternatives, (206) 875-5526
Stevenson: Skamania County Council on Domestic Violence,
   (509) 427-4210
Sunnyside: Lower Valley Crisis and Support Center,
   (509) 837-6689
Tacoma: Women's Support Shelter, (206) 383-2593
Walla Walla: Community Abuse and Assault Center,
   (509) 529-3377
Wenatchee: Domestic Violence Center, (509) 663-7446
Vancouver: Safe Choice (YWCA), (206) 695-0501
Yakima: Family Crisis Program (YWCA), (509) 248-7796

West Virginia
   Beckley: Women's Resource Center, (304) 255-2559
   Charleston: YWCA Domestic Violence Center, (304) 340-3550
   Elkins: Women's Aid in Crisis, (304) 636-8433
   Fairmount: HOPE, (304) 367-1100
   Huntington: Branches, (304) 529-2382
   Keyser: Family Crisis Center, (304) 788-6061
   Lewisburg: Family Refuge Center, (304) 645-6334
   Martinsburg: Shenandoah Women's Center, (304) 263-8522
   Parkersburg: Family Crisis Intervention Center, (304) 428-2333
   Wheeling: YWCA, (304) 232-0512
   Williamson: Tug Valley Recovery Shelter, (304) 235-6121

Wisconsin
   Statewide Hotline: 1-800-956-6656
   Milwaukee Task Force on Battered Women, (414) 643-5455
   Dane County: Advocates for Battered Women, Madison
      (608) 251-4445
   Eau Claire: Refuge House, (715) 834-9578
   Elkhorn: Association for the Prevention of Family Violence,
      (414) 723-4653

Greenbay: Task Force Against Family Violence, (414) 432-4244
Janesville: YWCA Alternatives, (608) 752-2583
Kenosha: Women's Horizons, (414) 652-1846
La Crosse: New Horizons, (608) 791-2600 or (608) 791-2610
Ladysmith: Time Out, (715) 532-6976
Manitowoc: Domestic Violence Center, (414) 684-5770
Marinette: Rape and Domestic Violence Center, (715) 735-6656
   or (715) 735-6657
Marshfield: Crisis Line, (715) 421-2345
Menomenie: Domestic Abuse Project, (715) 235-9074
Milwaukee: Milwaukee Women's Refuge, (414) 671-6140
   Task Force on Battered Women, (414) 643-5455 (days only)
   Sojourner Truth House, (414) 933-9565
Ozaukee County: Advocates Helping Battered Women,
   (414) 375-4034
Platteville: Family Advocates, (608) 348-5995
Racine: Women's Resource Center, (414) 633-3233
Rhinelander: Council on Domestic Violence, (715) 362-6800
Richland Center: Passages, 1-800-236-4325
River Falls: Turning Point, (715) 425-6751
Sturgeon Bay: HELP of Door County, (414) 743-8818
Viroqua: Domestic Abuse Project, (608) 637-7052
Wausau: Crisis Line, (715) 842-5746 or (715) 842-7323
West Bend: Friend for Battered Women, (414) 334-7298

Wyoming

Albany County: SAFE, (307) 745-3556
Big Horn County: Family Violence and Sexual Abuse,
   (307) 548-6543
Campbell County: Gilllette Abuse Foundation, (307) 686-8070
Converse County: Converse County Coalition, (307) 358-4800
Crook County: Family Violence and Sexual Assault Services,
   Sundance, (307) 283-2620 or (307) 283-2415
Evanston: Sexual Assault and Family Violence Task Force,
   1-800-445-7233
Fremont County: Fremont Alliance, Riverton, (307) 856-4734
Goshen County: County Task Force, Torrington, (307) 532-2118
Hot Springs: Hot Springs Crisis Line,
   Thermopolis, (307) 864-2131
Johnson County: Johnson Family Crisis Center, 1-800-257-0911
Laramie County: Grandma's Safehouse, (307) 632-2072

Lincoln County: Turning Point, (307) 877-9209
Natrona County: Self Help Center, (307) 235-2814
Park County: Crisis Intervention Services, Cody,
  (307) 527-7801
Platte County: Project SAFE, Wheatland, (307) 322-4794
Sheridan County: Women's Center, (307) 672-3222
Sweetwater County: Safe House Program (YMCA), (307) 382-6925;
  (307) 875-7666 in Green River
Teton County: County Task Force, (307) 733-7466
Vinta County: SAFV, (307) 789-7315
Washakie County: Confidential Assistance Line, (307) 347-4991
Weston: FOCUS, Newcastle, (307) 746-3630
Reservation: Circle of Respect, (307) 332-7046

IF SHE HAS A DRINKING OR DRUG PROBLEM AND WANTS TO GET IT UNDER CONTROL:

Call the Council for Alcohol/Drug Abuse listed in her local phone directory.

Call the Alcoholics Anonymous chapter listed in her local phone directory.

Call the National Alcohol and Drug Helpline, 1-800-821-4357. A courteous, professional counselor will listen and refer her to the people in her town who can help. Even if she is broke, out of work, and out of luck, they can help by referring her to the agencies that can help her at little or no cost.

Call the Cocaine Hotline, 1-800-262-2463. This is a national Drug Abuse Treatment Referral and Information Service, and is available twenty-four hours a day, seven days a week.

Call 1-800-ALCOHOL (information and referral only).

Also in Alabama, call HELP (Help Eliminate Lawbreaking Drug Pushers), 1-800-392-8011.

IF SHE IS HURT, BRUISED, BLEEDING OR IN PAIN, IF SHE HAS A BROKEN BONE, IF HER HEAD HURTS OR IF SHE HAS DIFFICULTY SEEING, SWALLOWING, TALKING OR SPEAKING AFTER A BATTERING ATTACK:

She should call her family doctor, her pediatrician, her gynecologist or obstetrician at once.

If she does not have a physician she can reach right away, she can go to the nearest hospital emergency room and ask for help. If she explains that she is a battered woman, the emergency room staff can arrange for a crisis center counselor to visit her while she is in the hospital. She must tell the counselor the truth about what has been happening to her.

If she has no transportation, she should call an ambulance, the police, the fire department, or the local 911 emergency help line. What she should *not* do is wait. *She could die.*

IF SHE THINKS HE HAS GIVEN HER A DANGEROUS DISEASE:

She should tell her family doctor, her pediatrician, her gynecologist, or her obstetrician, or go to the nearest emergency room. Everything she tells the physician will be kept confidential.

If the man in her life will not allow her to go to the doctor, she should at least make a call.

She can call the AIDS Hotline, 1-800-342-AIDS. This free national service is operated by the American Social Health Association twenty-four hours a day, seven days a week. The well-trained, courteous counselors can direct her to appropriate resources among 8000 entries in their database.

She can also call the ADIS Information Hotline for additional information. 1-800-590-2437.

Additional help and information are available in many states.

Arkansas
Call AIDS Information, Little Rock, (501) 375-5504.

California
Contact The AIDS Health Project, Box 0884, Dept. P, San Francisco 94143.

Georgia
Contact AIDS Atlanta, 1132 Peachtree St., N.W., Dept. P., Atlanta 30309.

Louisiana
Call AIDS Hotline, New Orleans, 1-800-992-4379.

THE BATTERED WOMAN'S SURVIVAL GUIDE

Massachusetts

Contact AIDS Action Committee, 661 Boylston St., 4th Floor, Dept. P, Boston 02116.

New York

Contact American Foundation for AIDS Research, Box AIDS, Dept. P, New York City 10016.

Call the AIDS Prevention Line (716) 847-4520.

Texas

Contact AIDS Foundation Houston, 3927 Essex Lane, Dept. P, Houston 77027.

Call the CDC's STD Hotline, 1-800-227-8922, for information and referral to a nearby health care agency.

Call the Health Information Center, 1-800-336-4797.

IF SHE NEEDS JOB COUNSELING:

Call an office of her State Employment Commission.

IF HE'S ABUSING THE CHILDREN:

Call the National Child Abuse Hotline, 1-800-422-4453.

Additional resources are available within some states.

Arkansas

Call Child Abuse and Neglect, Little Rock, 1-800-482-5964.

Florida

Call Parents Anonymous, Tallahassee, (904) 488-5437.

Illinois

Call Child Abuse Prevention, Springfield, (217) 522-1129.

Indiana

Call State Child Protection Service, Indianapolis,
(317) 232-4420.

Maryland

Call People Against Child Abuse, Annapolis, (410) 269-7816.

Michigan
Call Child Abuse and Neglect, East Lansing, (517) 887-9450.

Pennsylvania
Child Abuse Committee of Greater Philadelphia, Philadelphia, (215) 864-1080.

Texas
Call the Child Abuse Hotline, 1-800-252-5400. Counselors answer this number twenty-four hours every day. They understand both child abuse and battered women and will try to help her and her children.

Call Heartline, the hotline for Parents Anonymous of Texas, 1-800-554-2323. Although this number will be answered by a trained volunteer in Austin, Parents Anonymous has sites in twenty cities across the state.

Heartline's counselors will preserve her confidentiality. They won't ask for her name or address or any other personal information about her unless she wants to tell them. If she is ready to leave the battering situation, they will refer her to a battered women's center or family crisis center in her area. If she is not, they will talk about alternatives that can help her. If she likes, they can even contact a Family Outreach Worker in her area, who can come to her with direct, personal help. And if she or her children are in danger, they will stay on line with her and call the police or sheriff to go to her.

IF SHE NEEDS HELP FOR ADOLESCENTS, OR IF SHE IS A TEENAGE BATTERED WOMAN:

Call the Runaway Hotline, 1-800-392-3352. This national hotline for runaways or the parents of runaways is supported by the Department of Justice in Texas and is answered twenty-four hours a day, seven days a week.

Call the National Center for Missing and Exploited Children, 1-800-843-5678, to report on or find a runaway or find transportation home for a runaway who wants to go home.

Call Child Find of America, 1-800-426-5678.

Call the Missing Children's Help Center, 1-800-872-5437. They can provide advice, take information, and help provide

THE BATTERED WOMAN'S SURVIVAL GUIDE

transportation home. They also distribute photographs of missing children to help identify and locate them.

Call the national office of Toughlove International, (215) 348-7090 to find ways to help troubled teenagers help themselves.

Additional assistance is available within the states.

Texas

Call Heartline, the Hotline for Parents Anonymous of Texas, 1-800-554-2323. Their trained counselors will listen and offer advice about how and where to get help.

Call Toughlove for information on how you can help teenagers to help themselves, (214) 358-4761.

Call the Missing Persons Clearinghouse, Texas Department of Public Safety, 1-800-346-3243. All state police organizations have a missing persons clearinghouse.

IF SHE NEEDS LEGAL ADVICE:

She should call the nearest family crisis center, because they are in contact with the local law enforcement agencies. Most are also in contact with attorneys who know all about advocacy for battered women. Attorneys who work with women's shelters understand when a woman tells them she has no money, and they will either help her anyway or help her reach Legal Aid or a Legal Services Office.

Call the nearest Legal Aid or Legal Services Office listed in the telephone directory.

Call the Women's Legal Defense Fund, (202) 986-2600, for referrals for lawyers nationwide.

On a state-by-state basis, other legal resources are available.

California

Call California Rural Legal Assistance, Salinas,
1-800-677-5221.

Call City Attorney's Domestic Violence Unit, San Diego,
(619) 533-5620.

Call District Attorney's Domestic Violence Unit, San Diego,
(619) 531-4062.

Call Legal Aid Society, San Diego, (619) 262-0896.

Colorado
Call Colorado Rural Legal Services, Denver, (303) 534-5702.

Illinois
Call Equip for Equality, Chicago, 1-800-537-2632.

Maryland
Call Legal Aid Bureau, Baltimore, (410) 539-5340.

Mississippi
Call North Mississippi Rural Legal Services, Oxford, 1-800-898-8731.

New Hampshire
Call New Hampshire Legal Assistance, Portsmouth, 1-800-334-3135.

North Dakota
Call Protection and Advocacy Project, Bismarck, 1-800-472-2670 (days only) 1-800-642-6694 (24 hours).

Texas
Call the County Attorney's office for hotline information.

Call the Lawyer Referral Service, 1-800-252-9690. A public service of the State Bar of Texas, this hotline can make referrals to lawyers who specialize in family law and to agencies that provide legal services for those who cannot afford a lawyer.

In Dallas County, call Lawyers Against Domestic Violence, (214) 748-1234 x3313.

Call Texas Rural Legal Aid, Weslaco, 1-800-369-0574.

Call Family Violence Legal Line, Women's Advocacy Project, for legal advice and information, 1-800-374-4673.

Virginia
Call the Virginia Lawyer Referral Service, 1-800-552-7977.

West Virginia
Call the North Central West Virginia Legal Aid Society, Morgantown, 1-800-794-5455.

THE BATTERED WOMAN'S SURVIVAL GUIDE

The battered woman *can* live a life that is free of pain, terror, and torture. She *can* find help. She *can* take charge of her own life. She *can* make a difference.

It's a long road back into the safe, sane, normal world, but she can find help, and with help, she can walk that road one step at a time. She can make the first step right now. All she needs to do is gather her courage and make that first phone call.